World Class

·CUISINE·

Other Books By Gail Greco

Great Cooking with Country Inn Chefs

The Romance of Country Inns

Tea-Time at the Inn

Secrets of Entertaining from
America's Best Innkeepers

A Country Inn Breakfast

Bridal Shower Handbook

◆

Companion to the Discovery Channel's Premier Cooking Show

World Class

◆ CUISINE ◆

Great Adventures in European Regional Cooking

Gail Greco

Photography by Tom Bagley

Photo Art Direction by Gail Greco

RUTLEDGE HILL PRESS
Nashville, Tennessee

Created under the auspices of Arna Vodenos Productions
(AVP), 131 Rollins Avenue, Suite 3, Rockville, Maryland 20852,
as a companion to the Discovery Channel television series,
World Class Cuisine.

Published in Nashville, Tennessee, by Rutledge Hill Press, Inc.
211 Seventh Avenue North, Nashville, Tennessee 37219.
Distributed in Canada by H. B. Fenn & Company, Ltd.,
1090 Lorimar Drive, Mississauga, Ontario L5S 1R7.

****

Book design by Kathy Whyte

****

Cover Photo by Tom Bagley
Art direction by Gail Greco
A view of the Acropolis from Filopappou Hill.
Recipes are Shrimp with Dill and Ouzo, and Pastítsio from
Symposio Restaurant in Athens.

****

Whisky selections and recipe wine and spirits pairings for Portugal,
Ireland, Scotland, and England sections:
Schieffelin & Somerset Co., New York, New York.
Greek wine and spirits selections from Greek Food and Wine Institute.

****

Recipes tested by Jo Sblendorio of Anjomark Studios, Ringwood, New Jersey,
and recipes from Portugal tested by Victoria Lowe of Washington, D.C.

Library of Congress Cataloging-in-Publication Data

Greco, Gail.
World class cuisine : great adventures in European regional
cooking / Gail Greco ; photography by Tom Bagley : photo art
direction by Gail Greco.
p. cm.
"Companion to the Discovery Channel's premier cooking show."
Includes index.
ISBN 1-55853-324-9
1. Cookery, International. 2. Cooks—Europe—Biography.
3. Hotels—Europe—Guidebooks. I. Title.
TX725.A1G6233 1995
641.59—dc20 94-34068
CIP

Printed in the United States of America
1 2 3 4 5 6 7 8 9 — 99 98 97 96 95 94

Contents

PORTUGAL

◆ CONTENTS ◆

SCOTLAND

GREECE

Bungalows by the Bay and Cretan Village Dining

An Athenian Legend Hosts the World

Little Meals

The Story of the Greek Meze

ENGLAND

The Muse of the Flambé and the Temptations of the Table

The Culinary Scents of Yesterday Stirred His Career

For Arna Vodenos,
an artist who creates masterful images on
the television screen and the artist's canvas —
bringing her brushstrokes to life for those she holds close

Special Thanks to:

Schieffelin & Somerset Co.

and

Greek Food and Wine Institute ◆ Guinness ◆ Porta ◆ Ulster Weavers

All recipes edited and tested for American kitchens

Discovering World Class Cuisine
A TV Crew Travels Big Cities and Back Roads

It was a misty night as our mini-bus rambled for hours through the narrow country lanes and past the quaint houses of the Portuguese villages that dot the east-central and Alentejo regions. Suddenly, out of the ethereal dusk rose a jagged-stone cutout in the sky ahead. It resembled a medieval walled city, and was silhouetted atop the crest of a mountainside — the light of the moon shining on it like a big searchlight from the heavens.

Could this be the Santa de Rainha Isabel, the famous pousada we were assigned to shoot?

Motoring closer, we could see that the castle — its towers standing stalwart but welcoming — was unquestionably the former fortress of a revered queen.

Our bus and equipment van were rolling up to another one of our many destinations — laden with miles of cables, cylinders housing tripods, crates of blank tape, and carry cases of all shapes and sizes jammed with lightstands, extra bulbs, still and video cameras, TV monitors, laptop computers, and pads of note paper. We were well prepared for our long

Director Richard Schreier (center) works with Chef Jacky Froger at the Grande Bretagne in Athens. From left: videographer Paul Young, field producer John Marshall Meyers, and videographer Tony Cunningham.

journey in search of the world's best cooking and the wonderful and talented people who create it.

World Class Cuisine was once again on the road, photographing the culinary secrets of the world's top kitchens to bring them into the living rooms of millions of viewers everywhere. And as we turned each new corner on a trip that would take months, an open door and a surprise awaited.

In our quest, we aimed to reflect the look and the culture of each country on the

Author Gail Greco is surrounded by Chef Helmut Ziebell (third from right) and his staff at the Ritz in Lisbon.

dinner plate. We wanted to focus on the people — those in famous cities and quiet country towns — who make dining rooms everywhere romantic and sumptuous places to satisfy the palate.

At our destinations this season — Portugal, Ireland, Greece, England, and Scotland — we poked in and out of small towns, worked at the stoves of busy and prestigious kitchens, gathered recipes, and picked produce with the chefs. We visited a mustard maker and farmers of everything from mussels to mushrooms; saw how salmon is smoked and sugar plums are made. We learned how to make a proper cup of tea, only minutes from the queen's parlor at Buckingham Palace; saw how wine bottles are corked by hand in a cellar where it's been done that way for more than sixty years; discovered how to cook with renewed spirit by stirring in Scotch whisky or kneading the renowned brown bread for a bounteous Irish breakfast; and sat at tables where we experienced the Greek *meze*, eating *little meals* for supper.

We were also beneficiaries of the wonderful culinary trend that is revolutionizing fine cuisine across the United Kingdom. No longer is the fare of this region meat and potatoes. The cooking is sophisticated with French overtones and regional strengths. As author Mike Bunn sums up in his book, *Ireland: The Taste and the Country,* "If most of the new breed of Irish chefs continue to practice their calling here, Irish cuisine will have exerted a deep and distinctive influence on the world of gastronomy. As the superlatives ascend in describing the quality and imagination of the new cooking, go out again and again to backwaters, the cottage restaurants, the country houses, the small hotels, and farms of Ireland to discover a rose in the stew."

We visited famous food suppliers and dinnerware makers. Our cameras caught the ubiquitous Irish drink *Guinness Stout* direct from the distillery as it settled in pint-size glasses. We marveled at the painstaking work of the artisans at Waterford Crystal. We were charmed by the success of small entrepreneur Nicholas Mosse, who — working from his potter's wheel on the banks of a picturesque river in Ireland — is hand-throwing a commissioned line of dinner-ware for Tiffany's.

The desire to share these culinary revelations and their complementary environments spurred us on to capture it all on tape for viewers and here in print for you to enjoy, too.

Bringing viewers and readers the news and how-to information about food fashion was also at the heart of our desire to delve into the culinary philosophies of the great chefs and absorb their knowledge for home kitchens.

Behind the scenes, the world's best kitchens look similar. But the large stainless steel countertops and stoves are merely blank canvases upon which are designed a multitude of crisp new dishes with the styles and techniques brought to them by myriad personalities.

Although each chef has his or her own methods and ideas, some common elements kept emerging. Today, diners — whether eating in the shadow of the Parthenon, near the banks of the Douro River that carries romantic port wine in oak casks, or by a cozy kitchen nook at home — are looking for the humble taste and food from that day's market.

"Fresh ingredients" is the rallying cry heard 'round the kitchens of the world. Whether the chefs receive produce directly from a local supplier or pick it themselves from rows of blooming herbs and vegetables in the garden right behind their restaurant, *fresh* is the credo everywhere high-quality cooking is served. This is the one thing, these chefs clamor, that makes their food so special, and is their most repeated piece of advice to the home cook. They are ever so proud of being able to serve the freshest foods.

Another message circulating everywhere from Portugal to England is that food must be kept simple, especially nowadays with the emphasis on health and lighter fare. The chefs are emphatic about bringing out the flavors in their cooking rather than dwelling on heavy sauces and complicated recipes. There is a return to basic, rustic, and traditional cuisine, "a hunger for cooking that reminds us of home," and a desire to "make food that nourishes." That's how some of the chefs have described it. Today's culinary mentors have reached beyond the old obsession with developing something never done before. Rather, they concentrate on creating the timeless and the inherently good.

So what is world class cuisine? Quite frankly, it is — in its newfound simplicity — classier than ever, because the chefs of all these nations have shown us that today's world class cuisine is really farmer's market cuisine mixed with an intrepid teaming of ingredients, sterling culinary techniques, and the essence of art on the plate. It is magnanimous yet humble cuisine — pure, forthright, and highly principled with only the noblest of intentions. You can hear the excitement in their voices as these chefs passionately explain what the abundance of raw ingredients means to them today.

You will find these culinary beatitudes

throughout this cookbook in the words of the chefs themselves. And you will see them in the recipes, which were chosen to reflect the new attitudes as well as the culture of each country. With so many different styles, my metiér as a food editor was to make it all work together for you the reader. I selected recipes at easy and moderately challenging levels so that you could choose, depending on your mood and available time. I also selected classics cooked in new ways so that you could bring foreign flavor onto your stove. I know that you will truly enjoy these recipes as I did sampling all of them on the road. Then my choices were all reaffirmed by our recipe testers, who kept writing in red on the test sheets: *delicious, delicious, delicious!*

I traveled nearly 10,000 miles by road and many more by air with the crew of *World Class Cuisine* to find the best a country had to offer in the way of cooking at country houses, cottage restaurants, and luxurious hotels. These places, with their meritorious credentials, are barometers of what we ultimately do in our own home kitchens. And ironically, you and I, the travelers, feed the chefs our desires by what we order from the menu. They respond, showing us how to do it even better at home.

As the *World Class Cuisine* vans parked at their final destination for this season, the crew unloaded the miles of cables, slightly more worn now; the carry cases of spare bulbs, now lighter; and of course the shot tapes, stacked like countless volumes of an encyclopedia with their tons of colorful culinary images.

But what weighed most in our minds were the memories and souvenirs we brought back. They were tokens in the spiritual sense of great cooking adventures where we shared not only knowledge and hard work, but also friendship and good taste with the chefs and many others.

In their words, we wish you, as they did us, good health — or *ya sou* as they said in Greece, *cheers* from England, *flainthe* from Scotland, *flainte* from Ireland, and *a vossa saude* from Portugal. ◆

Gail Greco

The gleaming round domes of silver butlers bob up and down in the hands of servers in dining rooms around the world, such as here at Marlfield House.

In Appreciation

Upon my return from our final trip for *World Class Cuisine,* a friend wanted to "see the vacation pictures." I told her very nicely that although we used cameras every day, there were no family albums to fill here. Working on the road for the cookbook and the television show filled the hours with little time to sightsee. The venues and the environment where we traveled were full of wonderful memories. But "the family album" is comprised of the places where we stayed, the meals we sampled, and the people we met. And they are all on the airwaves and in this cookbook. We worked long days in the kitchens and in the field, and were often exhausted on travel days. That is why I want to take this opportunity — on behalf of the entire *World Class Cuisine* team — to thank all of the people and places we visited for helping to make our job easier and giving us a home on the road. There are too many to mention here but these cannot go unheralded:

Mary Bowe from Marlfield House for treating us as though her family had come to visit. She gave us the best of everything.

The people at **Longueville House** for their constant work and understanding of our schedule changes and **Chef William O'Callaghan** for taking us to his favorite place to enjoy his world and hear him belt out an Irish ballad.

Frances Brennan at Park Hotel Kenmare for his candid opinions, great sense of humor, and gracious manner.

Luis Abilio for his energy, the personalized birthday cake, and fabulous Fado-singer send-off from his Santa Isabel that would have pleased the royalty who once lived at the pousada.

José Rodriguez do Santos and **J. Castro Ribeiro** from the Hotel Bussaco, who made sure we left with a wine from the year of our birth. Their humble and grateful manner changed each one of us in some small way.

Our driver in Portugal, **Joäo Carlos Bernardo,** who became a member of the team — pitching in at every turn from the mundane tasks to the problem-solving.

To the people of Krinos Foods in Greece and New York: **Ersi** and her sister, **Pepi Moscahlaidis,** for their chauffeuring and interpreting. **Evee Georgiadis** for her time on the set; and her husband, **Alexander**, for his tireless efforts in helping us climb to the top of Filopappou Hill — trip after trip — to bring the food, props, equipment, and well-laid plans to shoot the cover photo for this book. Evee's father, **John Moscahlaidis,** for his sensitivity and hearty meals; and **Irene Moscahlaidis** for running around the Plaka in her high heels, in the name of getting the job done. And most importantly, **Eric Moscahlaidis** of Krinos Foods in New York, for bringing us all together.

The people of the **Greek Food and Wine Institute** for pointing us in so many right directions.

Stavros Barbicas of Kourtakis Wines for his enthusiasm, guidance, and friendship.

Alecos Varsano for his savvy in getting us out of a jam and opening many doors we needed to unlock in Greece.

Porta porcelain for the use of their beautiful dishes in all of the Portugal recipe photos and **Ionia Pottery** for many of the dishes in the Greece pictures.

Nicholas Mosse of Mosse Pottery and his wife, Susan, for the gracious tour and afternoon

The World Class Cuisine *crew for Greece takes time out for a team photo at the ancient site of Delphi. From left: series director Richard Schreier, videographer Tony Cunningham, field producer John Marshall Meyers, show's executive food editor and cookbook author Gail Greco, videographer Paul Young, production assistants Dianna Vogel and Chapin Wilson, and cookbook still photographer Tom Bagley. (The Portugal team included producer Joe Martin, director Chuck Crawford, and videographer Dennis Boni. In the United Kingdom, videographer Sheila Smith, and production assistant Seth Bindler were on hand.)*

tea; the use of their pottery in our Ireland photos; and the dream-come-true romp through their seconds shop. **Denis Foley** for advancing us Mosse Pottery from his craft shop in Kenmare.

Tweedside Tackle in Kelso for the antiques and fishing props we were able to pair with food from Ednam House on the lovely banks of the River Tweed.

Ulster Weavers for the fabulous damask, and Irish tea towels and napkins we used in the ingredient shots for the TV show and in cookbook photos in Ireland and Scotland.

Schieffelin and Somerset's **Aura Reinhardt** for her faith and perseverance and **Jeff Pogash** for pairing wines with dishes for Portugal, Ireland, Scotland, and England, and for making the write-ups so inviting and romantic. **Kathy Spilotopoulos** of Nestor Imports for pairing the Greek recipes with Greek wines.

To the people at the Discovery Channel who work so hard with us, especially **Chuck Gingold** and **Emily Swengros Sullivan**.

And last but not least, **the chefs** for sharing their talents and for their spirit of cooperation and friendship. For trudging with us to their markets — often just before sunrise to meet our shooting schedule, and for insisting on making their kitchen ours.

My personal thanks goes to:

First and foremost, **Arna Vodenos,** the executive producer of *World Class Cuisine,* whose ardor, vision, artistry, and friendship, continue to inspire. She made it possible for the cookbook and television series to become reality.

Series director **Richard Schreier** for his warm and meaningful conversations with the chefs, his talent for projecting the essence of the story, and his passion for life.

Field producer **John Marshall Meyers** for his late nights at the fax machine and telephone to keep us on the right roads.

And the rest of the road crew I got to know: shooters **Paul Young, Tony Cunningham, Dennis Boni,** and **Sheila Smith.** Plus director **Chuck Crawford** and production assistants **Seth Bindler, Dianna Vogel,** and especially **Chapin Wilson,** a dynamic young philosopher and friend.

All of the folks at the production studio for their hard work and support, especially **Joe Martin** for his unfailing dedication, friendship, ability to make me smile in the middle of a script, and for his production work in Portugal. **Tricia Conaty** for her assistance with the cookbook. Post-production supervisor **Michael Chaparo,** who brought it all together, and everyone else back at the studio, who complemented our efforts on the road.

Kathy Whyte, my longtime designer and commercial artist, whose terrific "can-do" attitude has made dozens of my projects easier and more successful, including this one.

All of the recipe testers, especially **Jo** and **Tony Sblendorio** of Anjomark, for doing double duty and such conscientious work.

Trish Crowe, a dear friend and graphic artist, for her able hand in photo styling at Moyglare Manor in Ireland and in London. And a new friend, **Olivia Lichtig** of London, for also helping with photos there.

The **Mykonos** restaurant in Washington, D.C., and **L'Academie de Cuisine** in Bethesda, Maryland, for answers to culinary dilemmas.

Technical Photo in Lanham, Maryland, for reliable, high-quality color transparency film processing for this book.

Publisher **Larry Stone,** for his continued enthusiasm, sincerity, and excitement.

My **mother** for her incredible courage during a time when she needed me the most and I could help her the least. Thank you, Mom, for turning it around and helping *me* through.

And my husband, **Tom Bagley,** for his friendship, support, and of course, for the beautiful photographs. ◆

World Class

·CUISINE·

IRELAND

> **"**
>
> *When my feet first trod Irish soil I felt that I had come to a magic country and now, as I said goodbye, I knew it truly as an enchanted island.*
>
> **"**

DROMOLAND CASTLE'S BEDSIDE GREETING CARD

The monkfish at Park Hotel Kenmare

An eleventh-century round tower at Glendalough

Denis O'Neill serves
Irish coffee at
Dromoland Castle

Looking for Angels in the Castle's Dining Room

Chef Jean-Baptiste Molinari

The opening page of the bill of fare says a lot about the executive chef at Dromoland Castle: "The essence of art is patience and cooking is an art . . . The menu which you are about to sample has been carefully composed after months of research, tasting, argument, and despair, finally achieving a perfect balance of herbs, spices, and ingredients."

Chef Jean-Baptiste Molinari strives to please in his kitchen. Thus, there is always the struggle — the argument and despair — to achieve the desired balance, the perfect taste. In that search, he deigns to discover new creations, primarily French but with a sensitivity to Ireland. In fact, the menu includes Gaelic dishes, such as the Irish Farmhouse Vegetable Soup and the Hot Brown Bread Soufflé, all with Irish ingredients.

The ending to the special Irish meal on the menu is a true Irish Coffee, prepared for guests at tableside. A blend of whisky, sugar, strong coffee, and heavy cream, the famous drink was reportedly invented in the 1950s and served to transatlantic travelers during stopovers at one of Ireland's airfields: nearby Shannon Airport. A warm stem glass is coated with whisky so that later it will catch a flame and ignite the drink. Sugar is added, followed by a shot of whisky, and the two are stirred together.

The coffee is poured into the glass, followed by the cream, which is poured slowly over a spoon so that it floats on top. It is customary to drink through the cream rather than stirring it into the beverage.

Situated on 375 acres, Dromoland Castle dates to the sixteenth century. Gently rolling log fires help keep the castle warm while antique sculptures and paintings decorate the gallery and guest rooms.

Chef Molinari came to the castle from Monaco's Hotel de Paris where he worked for eight years and studied under world-renowned chef Alain Ducasse. Dromoland Castle has been put on the culinary map by Chef Molinari, who has brought it many awards. The chef learned cooking from his Italian father and grandfather, and Irish cookery in particular, from his mother. He was always with them in the kitchen, eager and curious.

"At seven years old, I'd be trussing the chicken. They stood me up on a chair so I could reach the counter," recalls a cheerful chef.

He loves blending the two nationalities. For example, he says, "I'm keen on pasta, so you see it on our menu a lot. I got that from my father, too. If he could have pasta with his morning cappuccino, he would."

A Lobster Fricassee with Spinach Tagliatelle is one of the chef's specials at the castle. Ireland is known for its seafood. "We have stormy weather in Ireland so the seas are turbulent. The fish struggle and swim harder, developing more muscles that lead to better flavor and texture," declares the chef.

His advice to cooks is to season a recipe as it cooks and not wait to add seasoning afterward. He also recommends steering away from the cheapest produce as taste suffers in the long run.

To Molinari, the flavor of his dishes is everything. "At the end of the day, you may have something to put upon a plate, but something isn't enough. Taste is what matters. Every time guests taste our food, we want angels to be dancing on the tip of their tongues." ◆

> *At seven years old, I'd be trussing the chicken. They stood me up on a chair so I could reach the counter.*

CHEF JEAN-BAPTISTE MOLINARI

Irish Farmhouse Vegetable Soup

There aren't many soups that are heartier or easier than this one, which is a modern version of the traditional Irish stew. It is delicious served as a starter for dinner or with a salad for lunch.

2	medium zucchini
2	carrots
2	whole leeks
2	small turnips
1	tablespoon butter
	Salt and pepper to taste
$^1/_2$	cup dried barley, soaked overnight
$^1/_2$	cup diced lamb
6	cups water, chicken stock, or broth
2	potatoes

Wash, peel, and dice the zucchini, carrots, leeks, turnips and potatoes. Set the vegetables aside.

Add the butter to a large saucepan and heat

continued on page 25

Irish Farmhouse Vegetable Soup is a castle favorite.

over medium-high heat. Add the vegetables, except the potatoes, and the barley and sauté until the vegetables begin to sweat. Season with salt and pepper.

Meanwhile, heat a small saucepan with enough water to cover the lamb. Blanch the meat and set aside.

Add the water, chicken stock, or broth to the vegetables. When the soup comes to a boil, add the diced potatoes and cook for five minutes. Add the lamb. Cook the soup for another five minutes. Add more seasoning if necessary and serve. Yield: 6 servings. ◆

Wine Suggestion

A dry, balanced sparkling wine such as this one, can cut through and harmonize with various flavors and textures found within the vegetables and meat. **Chandon Brut Cuvée** is a refreshing and elegant accompaniment to this classic Irish Farmhouse Vegetable Soup or to any fish, vegetable or meat dish.

The soufflé is in check at Dromoland. It's your move now.

Hot Brown Bread Soufflé

Brown bread is a staple of the Irish diet, making this soufflé most traditional. The inclusion of the pastry cream offers a moist dish and truly tasty soufflé. Use 3-inch soufflé dishes. The straight sides of the soufflé dish facilitate rising. Be aware that as soon as your soufflé is removed from the oven, the sweet will begin to deflate as the air trapped inside escapes.

continued on page 26

Pastry Cream:

- 1/2 cup fine sugar
-     Yolks of 3 large eggs
- 2 tablespoons all-purpose flour
- 1 pint milk
- 2 vanilla bean pods

Soufflé:

- 4 ounces brown bread, crumbled
- 4 teaspoons sugar
-     Whites of 5 large eggs
- 1/4 cup brown sugar
- 3 teaspoons lemon juice
- 1 tablespoon butter
- 1 recipe crème anglaise, see page 213 (optional)

Begin the recipe by making the pastry cream. In a medium-size mixing bowl, beat together the sugar, egg yolk, and flour.

In a medium saucepan, heat the milk just to boiling. Add the milk into the egg mixture along with the vanilla. Stir well. Pour into a saucepan and heat just to the boil. Pour into a large heatproof bowl and set aside. Remove the vanilla beans and discard.

Preheat the oven to 350°. Begin work on the soufflé by cooking the brown bread and the sugar in a small saucepan until deep brown in color. Cool. Set aside.

In a large bowl, whisk the egg whites until stiff peaks form. Add the sugar and lemon juice. Blend a

little egg white into the pastry cream. Gently fold in the remainder of the egg whites. Fold in the brown bread. Place in 4 individual ramekins that have been buttered and lightly coated with sugar. Place the soufflé in the oven and bake for 10 to 12 minutes or until puffed and golden brown on top. Serve with crème anglaise, if desired. Yield 4 servings. ◆

Spirit Suggestion

The subtle wood and honey flavors of **Hennessy V.S.O.P Privilège** — originally blended for the British royal family in 1817 — perfectly complement Chef Molinari's nutty-tasting soufflé.

From Banking to Baking and Irish to Asian in an Old Victorian

Chef Brian Cleere

PARK HOTEL KENMARE, KENMARE

On a cool, blustery, and fog-filled day, it is literally a warm welcome one finds upon entering the Park Hotel. A red-hot blaze in a tiny, rumford fireplace fed by wood and local black coal, greets guests. The little fire is always burning as the hotel's genuine symbol of hospitality.

The fireplace dates to 1897 when the Park

Hotel was constructed as a railway stop for the gentry visiting the still quaint and enchanting village of Kenmare, known for its lacemaking. Victorian elegance has left its mark on the traveler's stopover, which was saved and refurbished by present owner Francis Brennan. Brennan has decorated his hotel with prized country Irish and English antiques. Every common room is filled with something from his personal collection for guest use.

"I never want anyone whispering at the Park Hotel as though it were a place to just look at and not enjoy," says Francis. Even though the hotel has fifty guest rooms, "We operate it as though we have twelve," he proudly adds. The proof is on a wall of accolades that go from wine and culinary ribbons to five-star service and hospitality awards.

Brian Cleere has played a big part in some of those achievements. Born in Dublin the son of a banker, Chef Cleere started his career in the financial arena but followed his heart and pursued culinary training. Now, he vacations in foreign countries, learning new cooking styles. "My wife is Chinese and a great cook, and that has influenced my cooking as well," he notes.

When devising the menus, the chef consults with a local farmer who custom grows

Local fishermen bring Chef Cleere their bounty from the Kenmare River.

his produce. "Oftentimes, ingredients are only hours old when they hit the dining room," he says.

For a dinner party, Chef Cleere suggests, "Keep things simple and buy only quality ingredients so you can spend more time with your guests. You can't go wrong then."

His own inspiration stems from a spectacular dining experience at sixteen. He had his first grand dinner in County Waterford at the private castle-home of a family friend. "I knew from then on that I wanted to please people the same way," he recalls.

The chef's dining room — accented by antiques from an old headmaster's desk that serves as the service podium to some thirty different dining tables — is warm and exciting. Diners enjoy views of a tidal basin that ebbs and flows as the mountains across the water fill the picturesque window scenes.

It is this environment that sets the stage for the very eclectic dining at the hotel. The menu may host dishes such as Irish poached oysters, a French apple-and-cinnamon *Bavarois*, and a sea trout marinated in Oriental spices. The world is on your table at the Park Hotel. And now with Chef Cleere's recipes, it can be in your own kitchen. ◆

Original oil paintings grace the Park Hotel, such as this one in the main dining room. The antique sideboard hosts Chef Cleere's poached fruit in a lime and mint syrup. To make the dessert: poach a variety of 2 fruits each of mango, pears, plums, kiwis, 1 apple, and 8 strawberries, and make a syrup with 1 pint water, $^1/_2$ cup sugar, juice of 3 limes, and a cinnamon stick. Bring liquid to a boil and let thicken. Pour over sliced fruits. Discard the cinnamon.

Asparagus in Puff Pastry with an Orange Tarragon Sauce

Use the freshest, thin-to-medium asparagus spears for this rendition of a *feuillete* appetizer. It is quick and easy to prepare but has an elegant presentation.

1   egg, beaten
6   prepared puff pastry disks (about 3 inches round)
2   shallots finely diced
1   cup white wine
1   cup orange juice
1   cup heavy cream
48 thin asparagus
1   tablespoon chopped tarragon
      Salt and pepper to taste
2   tomatoes, blanched, skinned, seeded, and diced
4   sprigs chervil or flat-leaf parsley

Preheat the oven to 400°. Brush the pastry disks with the beaten egg. Set aside.

Meanwhile, begin the preparation of the sauce. In a medium skillet, sauté the shallots on medium-high heat in the wine and cook until the mixture reduces by two-thirds. Add the orange juice and reduce again, this time by one-half. When the orange juice and wine mixture has reduced, add the cream and allow the mixture to cook again over medium heat until it is further reduced, this time by one-third.

As the cream is cooking, blanch the asparagus in salted water and drain when cooked just slightly tender to the touch, about 4 to 5 minutes.

To assemble the dish, cut the pastry disks in half lengthwise, so that you have a bottom and a top. Place the bottom half of the pastry in the center of the plate. Add eight asparagus onto each serving plate, in a cluster fashion. Place the lid on top of the cluster, allowing the spears to fan out from the pastry.

Add the tarragon to the sauce and season with salt and pepper. Drape the sauce around the center of the plate. Garnish the dish with the diced tomato and the chervil. Yield: 6 servings. ◆

Wine Suggestion

SICHEL
FINE GERMAN WINES

GEWÜRZTRAMINER

QUALITÄTSWEIN
WHITE WINE · PRODUCT OF GERMANY

BOTTLED & SHIPPED BY
H. SICHEL SÖHNE GMBH, WEINKELLEREI, ALZEY, GERMANY
A.P.Nr. 5 907 209 012 95

ALC. 12.5%
BY VOLUME   PFALZ   750 ml

A dish such as the asparagus — containing flavors that are often difficult to pair with wine — is complemented well by **Sichel Gewürztraminer,** a robust dry wine. The spicy Traminer grape variety yields flavors reminiscent of cloves, lychee, roses, tarragon, and other soft herbs. The different layers of complex flavor that are found in this wine allow it to work well with preparations that include such diverse elements as orange juice, cream, tarragon, and asparagus, as in Chef Cleere's dish, or with hearty stews, casseroles, Chinese, and other spicy ethnic cuisines.

Grilled Medallions of Monkfish in a Ragout of Tomatoes and Capers

Monkfish has been called the "poor man's lobster," but this version, with its light and delicate sauce, offers an entree that is rich in flavor.

1 1/2   pounds fresh monkfish, cut into 12 medallions
         (4 per serving)
16   small shallots, peeled and finely chopped

3   tablespoons olive oil plus more for garnish
12 cloves garlic, blanched and then finely chopped
6   small ripe red tomatoes, blanched, peeled, seeded, and cut into quarters
2   tablespoons capers
    Salt and pepper
4   sprigs fresh rosemary

Rub each monkfish medallion lightly with olive oil. Cook the medallions on a grill, three minutes on each side. When done, set aside and keep warm. Prepare the vegetables.

In a medium skillet, heat the remaining olive oil (about 2 tablespoons). Add the shallots and sauté in the olive oil until just beginning to brown lightly. Add the garlic and cook until soft. Add the tomatoes and capers and heat through. Season with salt and pepper.

Drape the shallot mixture onto the plate and arrange the medallions of fish overtop. Drizzle each medallion with olive oil and garnish with rosemary. Yield: 4 servings. ◆

Wine Suggestion

A crisp and dry wine is required when pungent and acidic ingredients are called for in a recipe. The slightly smoky **Simi Sauvignon Blanc** has the character and backbone needed to stand up to a ragout of tomato and capers, and is a classic match with fish, shellfish, chicken or veal.

Chef Cleere's asparagus and monkfish sit atop one of the hotel's most-prized dining tables, overlooking Kenmare River.

Out of a 'Roaring, Screaming' French Kitchen, an Irish Chef Comes Full Circle

Chef William O'Callaghan

LONGUEVILLE HOUSE, MALLOW

*W*hen the first sweep of salmon runs up the Blackwater River, the O'Callaghans head for the smokehouse and change the menu at Longueville House. The river winds past their historic five-hundred-acre, wooded livestock farm and plush estate, providing the country house hotel with only one of its many sources of fresh cooking ingredients.

Oliver Cromwell, Lord Protector of the British Commonwealth, is said to have gone fishing in this same river during the seventeenth century when he battled landowners here. Reflecting on what must have happened to his ancestors, the chef's father, Michael, peers through a parlor window at one of Ireland's most scenic river valleys where his sheep now graze in the sunshine. "See the ruins of Dromineen Castle? Cromwell burned it, and took O'Callaghan land, but it's all back in our hands now," he says proudly.

Longueville House — with plaster-relief ceilings, crown moldings, and its individually appointed guest rooms — is one of Ireland's best country house hotels. It began twenty-five years ago when Jane and Michael O'Callaghan bought the property, tracing it back to their own family roots. They wanted it for the land and found the big Georgian-style house a burden until Jane decided to make it affordable by serving overnight guests. The farmers became innkeepers. That's when Chef O'Callaghan received his initial culinary inspiration.

"My mother did all of the cooking," recalls William. "She was after us all the time with a wooden spoon — to taste what she was making, that is. I grew up learning to love fresh food."

The garden is an integral part of Longueville heritage. William O'Callaghan, his mother, and his wife, Aisling, attend to it. The chef is poetic about his feelings: "The garden is the essence of our kitchen here. Without the garden, there is no kitchen."

To that end, he adds, "Respect food and be gentle with its preparation. Even when you do something as simple as wash lettuce, you must bathe it with your hands in a bowl, not push it under a running faucet."

Chef O'Callaghan trained under famed Chef Raymond Blanc (featured on page 176) for one year. "I woke up with nightmares of him screaming at me, but he was like a father, training you to be the best. Then I studied in a kitchen in France. It was a roaring, screaming kitchen. You had all to do to survive," recalls the chef.

William O'Callaghan faced up to his tough training and now serves some of Ireland's most creative, energetic, and flavorful dishes. No doubt, his propensity to persevere — like that of his family — paved the way for the excitement, the passion, and the peace he delivers to his dining room every romance-filled evening at Longueville House. ◆

Salmon-Mousse Ravioli with Prawns and Vegetable Concassée

Prawns are similar in appearance to shrimp, but they are larger and part of the lobster family with bodies shaped like Maine lobsters. In the United Kingdom, prawns are more popular than shrimp as they are sweeter and more delicate. If you cannot find prawns, substitute with langoustines or shrimp.

Dough:

1	pound all-purpose flour or semolina flour
4	eggs
2	teaspoons olive oil
2	teaspoons warm water
1	teaspoon saffron (optional)
1	teaspoon salt
1	egg white for egg wash

Salmon Mousse Filling:

4	ounces fresh salmon, skin removed
	Salt and pepper to taste
1	egg white
1/4	rib celery, finely diced
1/4	stick carrot, finely diced
4	leaves fresh basil, chopped
1/4	pound small prawn tails or shrimp, shelled and coarsely chopped
1/2	cup table cream

Prawns:

12	large prawn tails or large shrimp
2	tablespoons cooking oil

Concassée:

4	medium tomatoes
1	large zucchini, cut julienne style

In a bowl of electric mixer, add the flour, eggs, olive oil, saffron, and salt. Mix the ingredients together to form a ball of dough. Knead the dough

continued on page 34

Longueville House in the distance – as seen from the ruins of Dromineen Castle, originally part of the Longueville property

until smooth for about 4 to 5 minutes. Place in a bowl and cover with a tea towel. Refrigerate for 1 hour.

Meanwhile, prepare the salmon mousse filling. Slice the salmon into small chunks and place in a blender until coarsely chopped. Season with salt and pepper to taste. Next, add the egg white to give the mousse its airy and light texture. Set aside. Blanch the celery and carrot in a saucepan of boiling salted water for 2 minutes. Drain the vegetables and add them to the salmon mousse. Add the chopped basil. Mix in the chopped prawn tails. Stir in the cream. Refrigerate the filling for at least $1/2$ hour.

In a medium saucepan, blanch the large prawn tails in boiling water for 10 seconds then plunge them into ice water. Shell and keep refrigerated until needed.

To make the concassée, core the tomato, blanch in boiling water for 5 seconds, and then place into ice water. Peel the tomatoes and cut into quarters and then into small dice. Blanch the zucchini the same way. Reserve the $1/2$ cup water to use later for deglazing.

Return to the ravioli dough after the hour has passed. Divide the dough into 8 pieces. Using a pasta machine, roll out each piece of dough, sprinkling with flour to keep it dry. Roll it out to the second to the last thickness of the pasta machine, or if doing by hand, roll out to as thin as $1/8$ inch or thinner. Lightly egg wash a strip of dough. Place $1/2$ teaspoon of the prawn mixture at 2-inch intervals on the strip. When completed, cover with a second strip and press the top strip onto the bottom, around the mixture. Form each ravioli by cutting with a 2-inch round cutter,

discarding any excess dough around the cutter. You will get about 20 ravioli.

Preheat the oven to 375°. Place the pasta into boiling salted water for 4 minutes.

While the ravioli boil, heat the cooking oil in a large skillet. Sear the large prawns and place in the oven to heat through about 1 minute. Return to the skillet and deglaze the pan with $1/2$ cup of the water used to blanch the vegetables.

To assemble the plate, place 5 drained ravioli per serving around the plate. Pile a portion of the tomatoes and zucchini in the center. Add the prawns and pour the sauce overtop. Yield 4 servings. ◆

Wine Suggestion

The beautifully balanced **Moët & Chandon Brut Impérial** from France marries perfectly with fish and shellfish and helps to lend that 'special touch' to the grilled monkfish.

The chef's great-uncle, Archdeacon Jeremiah O'Callaghan, presides over his passion for horses and the chef's dish of Salmon-Mousse Ravioli with Prawns and Vegetable Concassée.

Fresh Lemon Mousse with Strawberry Coulis and Chocolate Sauce

Desserts with lemon provide a refreshing end to a meal, and this rendition is also light in taste and texture. It is easy to make and looks great on the plate.

Mousse:
- ³/₄ cup (about 8 lemons) freshly squeezed lemon juice
- Zest of 2 lemons
- ¹/₂ cup heavy cream
- 6 egg yolks
- ¹/₄ cup sugar
- 2¹/₂ tablespoons all-purpose flour
- Chocolate syrup for garnish (optional)
- 5 gelatin leaves or 4 tablespoons powdered gelatin

Meringue:
- 6 egg whites
- 1 cup sugar

Coulis:
- 1¹/₂ cups fresh strawberries, hulled
- 2¹/₂ tablespoons sugar
- ¹/₂ cup water
- 4 to 6 extra strawberries for garnish

In a small saucepan over medium-high heat, bring the lemon juice, lemon zest, and cream to a boil.

Meanwhile, in a large mixing bowl, whisk together the egg yolks, sugar, and flour until well incorporated. Pour the egg mixture into the saucepan when the mixture starts to boil. Turn the heat down to low and cook, stirring occasionally until the mixture comes together.

When the mixture has cooked it will be of pudding consistency. Add the gelatin, stirring the powder in well. Remove from the heat and set aside.

Prepare the meringue that will lighten the mousse. Heat the sugar in a medium saucepan until it caramelizes or is sticky.

Meanwhile, in a bowl of electric mixer, beat the egg whites until stiff peaks form. Pour the melted sugar into the egg whites while they are still beating. Turn down the speed of the beater and whisk until the meringue has cooled. Fold the meringue into the pastry cream mix.

Pour the mix into a wax paper-lined terrine pan. Place in the freezer until it hardens, about 2 hours.

While the mousse hardens, prepare the coulis. Make a syrup by melting the sugar in the water in a small saucepan over medium-high heat. When syrupy, pour into a blender or food processor. Add the strawberries and whirl until puréed. Pass through a sieve.

To assemble the dessert, cut the mousse, making ³/₄-inch slices. Place several slices onto a serving plate. Place them under a broiler for 1 minute, just to lightly brown the edges. Pour some strawberry sauce around the plate and top with a few fresh strawberries.

If desired, you can melt your own chocolate as Chef O'Callaghan does. Or use a prepared fudge syrup and decorate the plate, or simply add it to the strawberry sauce. Yield: 6 to 8 servings. ◆

Wine Suggestion

A slightly sweet champagne is necessary as a foil to the tart lemon mousse and the concentrated chocolate sauce. Traditionally, **Moët & Chandon Demi-Sec** is served with virtually any type of fruit dessert and is often used to bathe a fruit cocktail.

Guest rooms at Longueville sport antique beds, country linens, and in this one, a dessert of lemon mousse with strawberry sauce.

'Peasant Food' Is Royal Cuisine at Enchanting Castle

Chef John Sheedy

ASHFORD CASTLE, CONG

Cooking is like a World Cup soccer game to John Sheedy, chef at County Mayo's most majestic landmark: twelfth-century Ashford Castle. "It is not one ingredient that will make the difference in what you cook," he explains. "It is a series of moves that will make or break your dish, just like in soccer."

That is why he advises cooks — even chefs — to season their food. "A little lemon juice if needed, pepper, and maybe no salt. This sounds basic, but seasoning — and the correct amount — is very important to bring out flavors."

Chef Sheedy espouses the philosophy that good cooking means simple ingredients. "It is okay if a dish has many steps to prepare as long as its tastes are simple," he instructs. "You don't need exotic ingredients. Peasant food, if you will, put together so that it looks and tastes great, is the makings of a good recipe." He points to the terrine recipe here as a prime example of a sophisticated dish with many steps but great taste and simple ingredients.

He is also adamant about using fresh ingredients. Goat cheese he buys for the recipe that follows comes from a farm some thirty miles away. Chef Sheedy discovered the couple that owns the farm eight years ago and has been ordering their cheese ever since. (For more about goat cheese and recipes, see page 204.)

Sheedy's basic ideas hail to the chef's roots

in a small village fifty miles south of the bustling city of Galway. The chef was raised in a small hotel where his mother and father worked, wearing many hats from cook to maintenance worker.

"I watched my mother in the kitchen. She never liked using anything packaged. Whatever we had to eat and whatever she served hotel guests was made fresh," the chef recalls.

He began making his own culinary suggestions, and after awhile the chef's mother allowed her eager son to try his ideas. After culinary training and work as a chef at country house hotels, Chef Sheedy came to Ashford Castle. Purchased in 1852 by Sir Benjamin Lee Guinness, owner of the famous Irish stout-making brewery, the castle had come upon hard times during the Irish famine of 1845-49. Finding the area in a state of poverty, Guinness put in a drainage system and brought the castle back to life so that he could employ hundreds of Cong citizens. Guinness family collections still adorn the castle where guests can stroll along the shore of Lough Corrib — and enjoy a brush with royalty, imagining how life once was here.

There are four dining rooms, each with its own personality and some with Waterford crystal chandeliers. Silver butlers abound as do the human ones in black tails, aiming to pamper. Meanwhile, Chef Sheedy remains in the kitchen like a soccer goalie, making all the right moves to lead his team to culinary victory. ◆

The castle sits majestically on Ireland's second largest lake, Lough Corrib.

Goat Cheese Tart with Rhubarb Sauce

Ireland's goat cheese is superb, especially the cheese served at Ashford Castle and made only an hour away on a private goat farm (see page 204). This recipe can be served as an appetizer or as lunch along with a fresh fruit salad. Rhubarb is a popular Irish vegetable with a slightly sweet taste. You can make any fruit syrup of choice. The sweetness offers a wonderful complement to the mildly tart cheese.

4   leaves phyllo dough
$1/4$ cup butter, melted
    Black pepper
8   ounces goat cheese
1   tablespoon olive oil

Sauce:
2   ribs fresh rhubarb, sliced into 1-inch chunks
2   cups water
$1/4$ cup sugar

Garnish:
$1/4$ cup seasoned breadcrumbs
$1/2$ head leafy green lettuce, cleaned and shredded
$1/2$ cup vinaigrette dressing of choice
$1/2$ cup slivered almonds, toasted

Preheat the oven to 350°. Brush the phyllo leaves with melted butter. Season each leaf with black pepper. Fold the sheets of phyllo over once. (You will cut out 2 pastry disks together.) Use a 4 to 4 $1/2$-inch cutter to make 4 circles (1 circle per phyllo leaf). Brush another coat of butter on the phyllo circles. Place a 2-inch piece (2 ounces) of goat cheese onto the center of each phyllo sheet. (Note: There should be 1 inch of phyllo around the cheese so that the dough can be folded up the sides of the cheese.)

Brush a layer of olive oil onto a 9x13-inch baking sheet. Fold up the phyllo around the sides of the cheese, brushing with more butter, if the dough needs moisture to stay pliable.

continued on page 41

Near the lake marsh that brushes the castle walls is a serving of the chef's Goat Cheese Tart with Rhubarb Sauce.

Bake the tarts in the oven for 20 minutes or until the pastry has turned a golden brown.

While the pastry bakes, prepare the sauce. Add the rhubarb to a medium saucepan with the water and sugar. Bring the water to a boil and turn down to medium high. Cook the rhubarb for about 4 or 5 minutes or until tender. Remove from the heat and set aside.

Remove the cooked tarts from the oven and sprinkle breadcrumbs overtop each one. Return to the oven for 2 minutes more, or just enough to lightly brown the breadcrumbs.

When ready to serve, spoon some of the sauce onto each serving plate. Place a tart in the center. Toss the lettuce with the dressing and place around the tart. Sprinkle toasted almonds overtop. Yield: 4 servings. ◆

Wine Suggestion

This softer style of champagne offers a fullness of texture and flavors that accent the tang of the goat cheese and the sweetness of the rhubarb sauce. **Moët & Chandon Demi-Sec** can be served as an apéritif, with sweeter foods and with flavorful or spicy dishes.

Vegetable and Lentil Terrine with Sage Mousse

A terrine is a molded, pâté-style food, usually served as an appetizer. The gelatin helps mold the dish in a long, narrow, loaf-style pan, called a terrine. Chef Sheedy said it took him months to create this recipe to his satisfaction. This will take only an hour or so of actual cooking time, but you will need to start two days ahead of time to soak the legumes, prepare the bacon (Irish preferred, see page 217 under Shannon Traditional listing), and then let the terrine mold. The mousse is optional but it is easy to do and offers a splendid accompaniment to the terrine.

Terrine:
- 1 ¼ cups brown lentils
- 1 ¼ cups black-eyed peas
- 1 bacon shank (ham hock)
- 1 ½ cups chicken stock
- 1 red pepper, roasted and cut into thin strips
- 2 leeks, white part only, blanched
- 1 large carrot, diced
- 1 medium zucchini
- ¼ cup vinaigrette dressing
- 6 large cabbage leaves, blanched, large center veins removed
- 2 tablespoons powdered gelatin
- Olive oil for glazing

Mousse:
- 1 teaspoon olive oil
- 1 bunch fresh sage leaves
- 1 teaspoon green mustard or substitute with a grainy mustard
- 4 hard-boiled eggs

On the day before, soak the lentils and peas in water separately (about 24 hours). Also, cook the bacon shanks or ham hocks in the chicken stock for 3 hours. Trim the meat off the shank, cutting it into

continued on page 42

strips. Set aside. Keep the stock but discard the shanks. Roast the red pepper (see page 209) and blanch the leeks.

On the day of preparation, cook the lentils and peas separately in unsalted water, enough to cover, until they are softened and cooked, about 20 minutes. Cook the carrot and the zucchini in water in another saucepan until they are tender, about 15 minutes. Drain and cool the legumes and mix them together in a bowl with ¼ cup vinaigrette dressing. Set aside. Drain the vegetables, cool, slice, and set aside.

Line the terrine pan with plastic wrap so that enough of the plastic spills out over the sides of the terrine to the bottom. Line the terrine with the cabbage leaves, so that they too spill out over the sides of the pan.

To build the terrine, add a layer of the lentil-pea mixture on the bottom of the pan. Follow with a layer of the carrot, zucchini, red pepper, and the pork. Add another cup or so of the legumes mixture,

pressing down to compress the food. Add a layer of red peppers and then a layer of leeks. Add another layer of zucchini, carrot, and pork.

Heat the chicken and bacon stock (reserved earlier) in a saucepan and add the gelatin, cooking until the liquid thickens and just lightly coats the back of a spoon. Add most of the stock to the terrine and press down lightly with your fingers to pack the terrine well. Add a final layer of zucchini, carrot, and pork and then a blanket of lentils and peas. Pour in the remaining stock. Brush cabbage leaves lightly with oil and fold them over, covering the top of the terrine. Cover all with plastic. Let set in the refrigerator for 5 hours or overnight.

When ready to serve, garnish with a quenelle of sage mousse on the side. To make the mousse, pour the olive oil, sage leaves, mustard, and eggs into a food processor. Blend until thickened and smooth. Form into little footballs or quenelle shapes. Yield: 10 servings. ◆

The Vegetable and Lentil Terrine with Sage Mousse in the private dining room at Ashford Castle

Wine Suggestion

Blue Nun Liebfraumilch from Germany is delicate with floral overtones and a hint of sweetness, making it versatile with food. The combination of lentils, peas, ham hocks, zucchini, carrots, and cabbage blends beautifully with the rich fruit of the wine.

At Home with Hammer or Whisk

Chef Gerard Costelloe

ADARE MANOR, ADARE

*W*hether he's installing a new staircase in his country farmhouse or mixing eggs with sugar for a peach tart at elegant Adare Manor, Chef Gerard Costelloe is right at home.

"In school, I hated to study. But I could turn out almost anything with my hands," recalls the chef. "My teachers wanted me to become a carpenter, mechanic, or woodworking instructor." However, Gerard discovered as early as fifteen that he was as handy with kitchen utensils as he was with handyman tools. He was so quick to complete his dishwashing tasks each night at a restaurant in his hometown, that he volunteered to help with the cooking. Recognizing Gerard's talent, the head chef handed him a uniform and put him to work one night when the staff was shorthanded.

From that humble beginning, Chef Costelloe's career has taken him to the kitchens of major Swiss, German, and American restaurants. The first member of his family to broaden his career in foreign lands, the chef is now back in familiar territory — just a few miles south of family and friends in Limerick.

Today as executive chef, Gerard heads his own busy Adare Manor kitchen brigade, which includes his wife, Eithne, the manor's pastry chef. The two met in culinary school and worked together before getting married two years ago. Last year, they bought a farmhouse just outside the picturesque village of Adare,

Today you can dine at Adare Manor, home to the Earls of Dunraven until the 1980s.

where Gerard is using his handyman skills to bring new life and charm to a long-neglected home. In the wee hours of the morning after a long day and night in the manor kitchen, Gerard and Eithne often can be found tackling the latest renovation project. From wallpapering to repairing walls or installing and staining that new staircase, they're re-doing the house from top to bottom.

Gerard sees common threads between cooking and carpentry. He believes he's good at both because he can concentrate on the job at hand while blocking out all else. His talents have won him a number of culinary awards and created a cozy home. In good weather, he and Eithne hop on their bikes and ride to the manor, often passing as many as fifty fox hounds out for morning exercise from a nearby equestrian center. Then it's on through the village of Adare — renowned as one of Ireland's prettiest thanks to the manor's landlord of the 1830s. The 3rd Earl of Dunraven bucked the trend of slate roofs and rebuilt the village with the charming thatched-roof cottages that still line its main street today.

The second and third earls also created a masterpiece of Gothic architecture in the manor house during the same period. And the family lived there until 1988.

But today the manor is home to the culinary masterpieces Chef Costelloe creates with those versatile and skilled hands. ◆

A thatched-roof Adare village cottage, as if in a dream.

Pan-Fried Roulade of Smoked Salmon and Goat Cheese with a Champagne Vinegar Salad

Easy is what comes to mind when you hear the word *roulade* — a thinly sliced piece of meat stuffed and rolled, baked, and put onto the table as though you had cooked for hours. Chef Costelloe offers this more unusual version of a potato crust stuffed with salmon and cheese, and served with a garnish of salad. It makes a great first course. Or, make larger portions for a delicious lunch. (See more on goat cheese on page 204.)

Roulade:

4   small Idaho potatoes, peeled and thinly sliced, about 1/4 inch or thinner

1/4   cup clarified butter
    Salt and pepper

6   ounces goat cheese

4   ounces smoked salmon filet

2   tablespoons cooking oil

Salad Garnish:

    Mixed salad of oak, radicchio, and green leaf lettuces
    Several twists of ground black pepper

2   teaspoons champagne vinegar or 2 teaspoons champagne mixed with 2 drops of red wine vinegar

1/4   cup hazelnut oil
    Salt and pepper

Preheat the oven to 350°. In a 9x13-inch baking pan, toss the potatoes with butter and sprinkle with salt and pepper. Bake them in the oven until tender but not brown, about 30 minutes. The starch from the potato and the butter will help the potatoes

continued on page 47

Salmon roulade before one of the more than fifty individually carved fireplaces that grace the manor

stick together so that they can form the outer crust of the roulade.

Prepare the roulade. Place the goat cheese between 2 layers (about 14 inches) of plastic wrap. Roll out the cheese until it forms a square and is about ¼-inch thick. Cut out a large square of aluminum foil (about 12x16 inches). Place the baked potatoes on the aluminum foil. Add the salmon and last the goat cheese. Roll up jellyroll style, keeping the food in the foil. Place in the refrigerator for 15 minutes or until ready to use.

Meanwhile, prepare the salad. Toss together the lettuce leaves. Twist the black pepper into a bowl and add the vinegar. Add the oil slowly and season with salt and more pepper. Set the dressing aside.

Remove the roulade from the refrigerator. Cut it into 4 equal portions. Heat the cooking oil in a medium skillet on high heat. Sear the roulade for about 2 minutes on each side. Place on a serving plate and add the tossed salad. Drape the dressing over the salad and let some of it pool to the side of the salad. Serve immediately. Yield: 4 servings. ◆

Wine Suggestion

WHITE STAR

MOËT & CHANDON

CHAMPAGNE

APPELLATION D'ORIGINE CONTROLÉE

ALC 12% BY VOL   EPERNAY ★ FRANCE   750 ML

FONDÉ EN 1743

PRODUCE OF FRANCE

Smoked salmon combined with pungent goat cheese in the roulade calls for the well-balanced richness of a champagne such as **Moët & Chandon White Star.** The complex Pinot Noir, Pinot Meunier, and Chardonnay grapes found in this wine create a sense of harmony and refinement.

Peach Tart with Saffron Ice Cream

Peaches are prolific in summertime, but you may substitute a number of fruits to make this dessert. Chef Costelloe's unusual ice cream employs saffron as it perfumes the ice cream with just enough flavor so as not to overpower the fragrant taste of the peaches. In medieval days, a pound of saffron cost as much as a house. Although not that dramatic, it is still expensive today, so substitute with turmeric.

Tart:

- 3 medium peaches, blanched and peeled
- ½ cup plus 1 tablespoon sugar
- ¼ cup water
- 4 3-inch circles of puff pastry, lightly pierced with a fork and baked at 400° for 15 minutes

Ice Cream:

- 2 cups plus 2 ½ tablespoons milk
- 3 ½ tablespoons, plus 2 teaspoons heavy cream
- 6 egg yolks
- ½ cup sugar
- ⅛ teaspoon powdered saffron

Preheat the oven to 350°. Cut the peaches into ½-inch segments. Place the sugar and water in a small saucepan. Cook over high heat until it boils. Lower heat to medium, and stir until a caramel syrup forms. Remove from the stove. Add the peaches to the pan and place evenly over the pastry disks. Bake in the oven for 15 to 20 minutes or until the peaches are tender and the pastry has turned a golden brown.

Meanwhile, prepare the ice cream. In a medium saucepan, bring the milk and 3 ½ tablespoons of the cream to a boil. While this is boiling, whisk together the egg yolks and sugar in a separate bowl. Pour the milk mixture into the bowl, except for 8 tablespoons that are set aside in another bowl for later use. Pour the larger portion of the milk and cream mixture back into the saucepan and cook for 2

continued on page 48

minutes. Strain the mixture into a bowl containing the saffron. The strainer helps rid the mixture of any egg yolk particles.

Place the bowl in the refrigerator until the mixture is well-chilled, at least 1 hour. Add the remaining 2 teaspoons of the cream and pour into the ice cream-making machine. Process the ice cream according to machine directions. Serve immediately with the peach tart and some of the reserved cream and milk or crème anglaise mixture. Yield: 4 servings. ◆

Peach tart atop the fifteenth-century Flemish choir stalls in Adare Manor's Long Gallery, proclaimed to be Ireland's longest room

What's for Dinner?
A Chef's Visit to a Mushroom Farm Has the Answer

Chef Jim Cullinane

MOYGLARE MANOR, MAYNOOTH

*C*hef Jim Cullinane likes to use simple ingredients in his cooking so that he can add a medley of flavorings. In fact, his policy and advice to the home cook is: "Do it nice and simple; make a light sauce; and don't go overboard."

Mushrooms are Chef Cullinane's favorite foodstuffs, because they allow him to invent a dish with herbs, spices, and other natural vegetable or meat flavorings. One of his mushroom soup recipes (see the Pantry section on page 209) is so good that it may also be used as a base for stews and casseroles.

It just so happens that not far from Moyglare Manor is a pioneering, organic mushroom-cultivating farm in County Kildare. Here, a sea of off-white button and breakfast mushrooms peer up from dark compost in darkened greenhouses. Ireland's temperate climate is ideal for the cultivation of mushrooms, which thrive on temperatures between sixty-five and sixty-nine degrees Fahrenheit in the controlled greenhouses. These greenhouses are literally just that — *green* in the ecological sense, but not in color. Natural waste resources from nearby farms are mixed with water and straw, and a natural fermentation process begins. The raw materials from the farms are thus converted into food that is placed into the large plastic bags where the mushrooms grow. Some two inches of enriched peat is placed on top of the compost to stimulate the fungus. After a three-week fermentation period, mushrooms will mature in about six days and are then ready for market.

That is when Chef Cullinane readies them for the soup pot or the baking dish — or in the case of the delicious Marinated Pork en Croûte with Mushroom and Bacon Duxelle, for the sauté pan. This delicious recipe incorporates the traditional duxelle, which is always a mixture of chopped mushrooms, onions or shallots, and butter.

The chef explains that a dish such as the mushroom soup is a signature of the house because, "It is lovely and light. That's what people want nowadays." The chef has been at the eighteenth-century, Georgian-style Moyglare Manor country house since 1983. But he has been cooking since he was fourteen.

"I grew up in east Cork near a fishing village — surrounded by fresh food. I think that was my real inspiration," he notes. Now, guests find Jim's food inspiring as they enjoy the elegant decor of this comfortable country house hotel. ◆

Smoked Chicken Salad with Tomato Chutney

A cold supper or an elegant lunch party can star this delicious salad combination. The chutney alone makes a wonderful addition to a variety of other salads and sandwiches.

Chutney:
- 1/2 *pound yellow onions*
- 3 *pounds ripe red tomatoes*
- 2 *cups sugar*
- 3/4 *teaspoon black pepper*
- 1 *tablespoon salt*
- 3 *cups cider vinegar*

Dressing:
- 1 *tablespoon peanut, walnut, or any nut oil*
- 1 *tablespoon olive oil*
- 1 *tablespoon sunflower oil*
- 1 *tablespoon vinegar*
- 1/2 *teaspoon Dijon-style mustard*
  Salt and pepper

Chicken and Salad:
- 1 *pound mixed lettuce*
- 1 *pound (cooked) smoked chicken or turkey, sliced*
- 1 *cup fresh-cooked and cooled beets, peeled and sliced*

Make the chutney first. Finely chop the onions into small dice. Blanch and skin the tomatoes, remove the seeds, and dice. In a medium saucepan, bring the onions, tomatoes, sugar, pepper, salt, and vinegar to the boil. Cook over low heat until you have a rolling boil. Cook until thick, about 40 minutes.

Prepare the salad. Mix together the ingredients for the dressing. Arrange the lettuce in the center of each plate. Add the chicken and beets and top with chutney. Pour the dressing over all. Yield: 4 servings. ◆

Wine Suggestion

The ripe strawberry flavor and creamy texture in this delightful dry **Clivo** from Ruffino beautifully complements this dish. The contrasting flavors of sweet chutney and smoked chicken require a wine with ripe fruit flavors and good structure.

The manor's foyer provides the perfect spot to enjoy a good book, a fine wine, and the smoked chicken.

Marinated Pork en Croûte with Mushroom and Bacon Duxelle

Prepare this recipe a day ahead of time so that the pork can marinate. The duxelle combines mushrooms and butter with flavorings to form a mushroom paste. This duxelle introduces the unusual and flavorful bacon in its midst. Irish bacon is best (see page 71). This is an appetizer for four, but you can make it a meal for two. Serve with a little applesauce.

Marinade:
2   boneless butterfly pork chops or slit pork steaks
¼   cup olive oil
2   tablespoons lemon juice
    Salt and pepper
2   bay leaves

Duxelle:
2   ounces bacon, chopped
1   tablespoon butter
¼   pound button mushrooms, chopped
2   tablespoons chopped onions
½   teaspoon parsley
½   teaspoon thyme
    Salt and pepper

Croûte:
1   sheet puff pastry
1   egg, beaten for egg wash

Combine all of the other ingredients for the marinade in a glass baking dish and let the pork marinate in the refrigerator for at least 8 hours or overnight. Turn often, coating the pork well.

Next day, prepare the duxelle. In a no-stick skillet, sauté the bacon in the butter until cooked tender. Add the other ingredients and sweat lightly. Allow the liquid to reduce by ⅓. Remove from heat and let cool. The mixture should hold together like a paste.

Preheat the oven to 350°. Roll out the pastry to ⅛-inch thickness. Cut in half. Remove the pork from the refrigerator. Stuff each pocket evenly with the mushroom duxelle. Seal the pastry around the pork with the egg wash. Bake in the oven for about 40 minutes or until the pastry is golden brown. Cut each piece in half, if serving 4 as an appetizer, or leave whole for 2 main courses. Yield: 4 appetizer servings or 2 main courses. ◆

Wine Suggestion

A single-vineyard Chianti Classico with deep fruit flavor and hearty structure, **Santedame** from the *Tuscan Estates of Ruffino* is the perfect accompaniment to pork, veal, chicken, and red meats.

A leprechaun amid the mushrooms at Moyglare

A classical combination: the filet of pork with mushroom stuffing in the parlor (For mushroom soup recipe, see page 209.)

A Tearful First Day on the Job and a Culinary Spy in the Cellar

Chef Michel Flamme

THE K CLUB, STRAFFAN

The soundtrack for *A River Runs Through It* — Robert Redford's movie about life and fishing in the wilds of Montana — was recorded halfway round the world in the city of Dublin. And scarcely 17 miles upstream from Ireland's capital, a modern-day story of a chef in love with fly fishing (as well as cooking) is played out by Chef Michel Flamme at the Kildare Hotel & Country Club, or K Club.

At the center of a bucolic view from the chef's dining room, the Liffey River bends its way through the K Club property on its way to Dublin, and you cannot help but recall images from the movie. Given a break from his cooking duties, Michel swaps his chef's toque for angling gear, wades in, and casts for the trout and salmon that populate the Liffey. (The fish you order that evening may truly be the chef's catch of the day!)

Even though he confides, "I cannot live without a daily fix of fishing," cooking is Michel's metiér. At age eight, he insisted on preparing the starter courses for his mother's dinner parties. Michel wanted to be a chef so badly that he spent his first trial day at a restaurant in his native France, peeling some one-hundred pounds of onions. "I cried all day but I got the job," he remembers.

His desire to learn also turned him into a bit of a spy. The head chef was secretive about some of his recipes and would lock himself up in the cellar to cook them. Although Michel pleaded with the chef to share these secrets, much to his chagrin, the chef was not willing.

Michel finally sneaked down to the cellar ahead of the head chef and hid so he could watch how it was done!

Chef Flamme's advice to the home cook is simple: "Keep it down to earth and remember that creativity comes naturally if you enjoy what you are doing. Don't cheat when you cook. Be true to the ingredients by letting their natural tastes come out."

The K-Club's Byerly Turk restaurant draws its unique moniker from a famous horse — for County Kildare is well-known as the "horsiest" region in all Ireland. Foaled in 1680, the Byerly Turk is one of three Arabs in the male line of every thoroughbred in the world! (The horse acquired his name from the colonel who rode him into battle after the stallion was captured from the Turks.) The entire entry wall in the restaurant is dedicated to a painting of the Byerly Turk by great English horse painter John Wooton (1678-1765). Horse breeding and racing abounds throughout the region. Post-and-rail fences line the narrow roadways as one picturesque horse farm fades into another.

From horsing around to fishing and of course, cooking, there is much going on along the Liffey — the most exciting of which is what's happening in Chef Flamme's award-winning kitchen. ◆

Unique ingredients in this special venison dish match the elegant furnishings at the K-Club.

Venison and Prunes with Pearl Barley and Celeriac Dumpling in a Port Wine Sauce

The barley is cooked with cream, almost giving the effect of risotto. This — along with the clean fresh taste of the dumpling laced with celery root and spinach, the rich ruby taste of the port wine, and the sweetness of the prunes — effectively complements the delicious venison. If venison is out of season in your area, check with your local butcher. He can usually order it for you, or you can substitute with veal. Don't let anything stop you from making this dish.

Dumplings:

1	medium celery root, peeled and cut into quarters
1/4	cup spinach leaves, blanched and chopped
1/2	cup cornmeal flour
3	tablespoons finely ground, skinned hazelnuts
1/2	tablespoon freshly chopped tarragon
1/2	teaspoon freshly chopped chervil
2	egg yolks
	Salt and pepper

continued on page 56

Barley:
- 2 cups water
- 2 tablespoons chopped shallots
- 2 tablespoons chopped carrots
- 2 tablespoons chopped celery
- 1/2 cup barley
- 1/2 cup heavy cream
- 1/2 cup butter
- 1 tablespoon chopped chives
- Salt and pepper

Venison and Sauce:
- 4 medallions of venison or veal
- 1 cup all-purpose flour for coating
- 2 tablespoons butter
- 2 tablespoons olive oil
- 1/3 cup port wine
- 1/2 cup chicken stock
- 4 prunes, stoned and cooked

Assembly:
- 4 large mushrooms
- 1 tablespoon butter

Cook the celery root in a small saucepan in boiling water for about 15 minutes or until tender. Drain and set aside. In another saucepan, blanch the spinach, drain, and chop. Add the tarragon and chervil to the spinach.

Prepare the dumplings. Mash the celery root and mix with the egg yolks, cornmeal flour, the spinach-tarragon mixture, and hazelnuts. Add salt and pepper to taste. Shape the dumplings with a spoon and poach in a medium saucepan of enough boiling water to cover for 3 to 5 minutes. Remove dumplings with a slotted spoon and set aside.

Prepare the creamy barley. Bring the water to a boil in a small saucepan. Add the barley and simmer for 45 minutes, uncovered. In a medium saute pan, sweat the shallots, carrots, and celery for 5 minutes. Add the cooked barley and cream, and reduce until thickened and creamy. Add the butter and chives, and season with salt and pepper to taste. Keep warm.

Season the venison with salt and pepper, and dip in flour, shaking off the excess. Melt half the butter with the olive oil in a large heavy skillet over moderate heat. Sauté the medallions for about 2 to 3 minutes or until golden brown on each side. Transfer to a plate and keep warm.

Drain off the excess fat from the skillet in preparation for making the sauce. Deglaze the hot skillet with the port wine, constantly scraping up the brown bits clinging to the bottom and sides of the pan (about 6 minutes). Add the chicken stock and boil until it is reduced to a syrupy glaze. Swirl in the remaining butter and turn off the heat.

To assemble, quickly pan-fry the mushrooms in the butter until browned. Place the medallions of venison on the serving plates. Top with a mushroom cap. Place a serving of barley on the side of the plate along with 1 dumpling per plate. Pour the sauce around the base and dress with a prune. Yield: 4 servings. ◆

Wine Suggestion

The venison is well paired with Ruffino's renowned and richly textured **Chianti Classico Riserva Ducale Gold Label,** a wine that displays a deeply concentrated ripe, black fruit character and finesse.

Mille-Feuille of Rhubarb and Mango Sorbets with Nut Wafer and Raspberry Sauce

Stacks of triangular biscuits form the layers for the mille-feuille. The unusual sorbets go in between and the raspberry sauce ties it all together. Before starting the recipe, make a template for the triangles (see tile preparation).

...creativity comes naturally if you enjoy what you are doing.

CHEF MICHEL FLAMME

Rhubarb Sorbet:
- 1 cup rhubarb, diced
- 1 cup boiling water
- 1 cup water
- $\frac{1}{2}$ cup sugar

Mango Sorbet:
- $\frac{1}{2}$ cup sugar
- 1 cup water
- 1 cup mango purée (1 mango)
- Juice of 1 lemon

Nut Wafer Batter:
- 1 tablespoon each: almonds, hazelnuts, pistachios, walnuts
- 1 egg white (large egg)
- 2 tablespoons powdered sugar

Tile Biscuits:
- $\frac{1}{4}$ cup all-purpose flour
- $\frac{1}{2}$ cup powdered sugar
- 2 tablespoons unsalted butter, melted
- $\frac{1}{2}$ cup egg whites (about 3 large eggs)
- 1 teaspoon vanilla extract

Sauce:
- $\frac{1}{2}$ cup fresh raspberries
- $\frac{1}{4}$ cup simple syrup (see page 213)

Assembly:
- Powdered sugar
- Heavy cream, optional
- Mint, optional

Prepare the rhubarb sorbet. Add the diced fruit to a cup of boiling water in a small saucepan. When fruit is tender, drain and purée in a blender. Make a syrup of the 1 cup of water and the sugar in a small saucepan, boiling until it thickens. Reduce the heat and add the rhubarb. Simmer about 5 minutes. Cool to room temperature. Freeze in an ice-cream maker, according to manufacturer's directions. Prepare the mango sorbet the same way but add the lemon juice after the syrup has cooled to room temperature.

Preheat the oven to 350°. Finely grind the nuts. Beat the egg whites until stiff peaks form; add nuts and the powdered sugar. Stir well. Pour batter onto a greased cookie sheet. Spread the batter out to about $\frac{1}{8}$-inch thickness. Bake for 12 minutes or until the biscuits are golden brown and dry to the touch. Remove from the oven; increase the temperature to 425°. Cool biscuit and crumble by hand or in a blender. Set aside.

Mix all of the ingredients for the tile into a mixing bowl. Set aside.

Make the triangle templates. Using a piece of $\frac{1}{8}$-inch-thick cardboard, cut a triangle, 7 $\frac{1}{2}$ inches on all sides. Measure $\frac{1}{2}$ inch from the edges and cut out the center. Cover the triangle with foil. Line a baking sheet with parchment paper. Place the triangle form on it and add about 1 $\frac{1}{2}$ tablespoons of the batter into the form. Smooth with a spatula until $\frac{1}{8}$-inch thick. Lift and continue making the triangles, adding the batter until all used up. (Note: The batter will remain in a triangle shape; slide the template off carefully.) You will have about 12 triangles. Sprinkle the nut

continued on page 59

Horse breeding is an art in County Kildare, as is Chef Flamme's fruitful dessert.

mixture overtop the batter in each triangle. Bake 5 minutes or until a rich golden brown. Remove immediately from the baking sheet and cool on wire rack. (Cookies are very fragile and when cooked will measure about 5 inches on all sides.)

Prepare the raspberry sauce by melting the simple syrup in the water in a small saucepan over medium-high heat. When syrupy, pour into a blender; add the raspberries. Whirl until puréed. Pass through a sieve. Set aside.

To serve, place a tile in the center of an individual serving dish. Shape the sorbets quenelle-style. Place one of each flavor on a tile. Add the second tile on top and place 2 more quenelles on the biscuit. Place a final tile on top. Sprinkle generously with powdered sugar. Add a dollop of raspberry sauce in several places around the plate. Add a couple of drops of heavy cream, if desired, and pull through with a toothpick to make decorative designs. Garnish with mint, if desired. Yield: 4-6 servings. ◆

Wine Suggestion

Sichel Eiswein
Flonheimer Adelberg

Estate Bottled by Wilfried Werner, D-6509 Flonheim

A sublime balance between rich, sweet fruit and lively acidity allows the **Sichel Eiswein** to harmonize with the rhubarb and mango.

The Kildare resort, home to the Byerly Turk restaurant and chef Michel Flamme's cuisine

A Garden in Bloom Outdoors and on the Plate

Chef Regis Herviaux

CASHEL HOUSE, CASHEL BAY

Beautiful but barren is the description often applied to Ireland's far west. Yet somehow — amid the countless rocks and lakes that dot this remote Connemara region — a marvelous garden flourishes where the sun shines indoors and out.

At Cashel House, herbs and flowers of endless variety grow in profusion and grace the recipes and dishes of Chef Regis Herviaux as well as the grounds here. Many of the gardens are the heritage plantings of a former owner of the house who believed anything can grow in Irish soil. And just about anything does.

Proprietors Kay and Dermot McEvilly enjoy their garden so much that they added a huge glass conservatory to the restaurant four years ago to "bring the outdoors inside." Now diners can have a ringside seat next to the many flowers that hug the front of the house.

Kay and Dermot's enthusiasm has been rewarded with numerous national gardening awards — including Best Overall Garden — from the Irish Tourist Board. In reality, their gardens are even more than a feast for the eyes. Diners can actually savor many edible flowers that appear on the chef's plates. In addition, an extensive garden of herbs and vegetables climbs a hill behind the house and supplies the kitchen. Guests can make their own ascension along the woodland walks at Cashel House to work up an appetite while admiring the many flowering shrubs — some imported all the way from Tibet. Rhododendrons, azaleas, camellias, and magnolias abound.

The restaurant also benefits from its position right on Cashel Bay. Fresh lobsters, mussels, clams, scallops, and salmon all come right from the local waters where Dermot keeps his boat at the ready. And Connemara lamb is another local treat prepared often by the chef.

The wonderful trout timbale, or seafood molded in custard-cup shape, is a favorite of the chef because it is easy to prepare and yet reflects the region. Chef Herviaux's versatility and sensitivity to trends is mirrored in the Yogurt and White-Chocolate Cheesecake. The mixture of yogurt into the cheesecake shows his concern for cooking lighter. This is one cheesecake you will not mind baking and enjoying in large portions.

The chef believes — as Kay and Dermot do — that "good food is food that you don't spend a lot of time on," thus allowing the natural tastes to come through.

The flowers and the meals from this young but in-tune chef, and a couple of innkeepers who seek poetry on their tables, make for a special place, full of life. Beautiful Connemara? Yes. But definitely not barren. ◆

Trout-and-Cheddar Timbales with a Lemon-and-Wine Cream Sauce

Easy and delicious, this makes a great appetizer dish or a luncheon plate. Substitute with smoked salmon if you cannot get the trout.

Timbale:
1 1/2   pounds smoked trout
1   cup heavy cream
1/4   cup grated Cheddar cheese

Sauce:
1   cup heavy cream
1   cup fish stock
1/4   cup white wine
    Zest of 1/2 lemon, finely chopped
1/4   teaspoon salt
    Black pepper

Garnish:
8 lemon slices
8 sprigs mint

continued on page 63

A trout-and-Cheddar timbale in the conservatory-style restaurant, where the garden and freshly cut flowers surround diners

Preheat the oven to 350°. Skin and break up the trout, making sure there are no bones. Place the trout in a medium skillet and add the cream. Cook over medium-high heat until the cream thickens. Stir frequently.

Butter 8 (2 1/2-inch) round ramekins. Pour the trout-and-cream mixture into the dishes and sprinkle with cheese.

Make a bain marie by placing the ramekins into a glass dish filled with water that goes halfway up the sides of the ramekins. Bake in the oven for 30 minutes or until the cheese is melted and lightly browned.

Meanwhile, prepare the sauce. In a medium saucepan, heat the cream, fish stock, and white wine, and allow to reduce by half. Add the lemon peel and sprinkle in the salt and black pepper. Stir.

When the timbales are cooked, pour sauce into the middle of the plate. Turn the trout and cheese timbale out in the middle of the sauce. Garnish with a lemon slice and a sprig of mint. Yield: 8 servings. ◆

Wine Suggestion

The Riesling grape, when planted in Germany, is perhaps the most distinguished of all varieties. Bursting with ripe-fruit character and having just the right level of crispness, this wine marries beautifully with the smoked trout. The **Lauerburg Bernkasteler Riesling Kabinett**, with its floral characteristics, makes an excellent accompaniment to all types of smoked fish.

Yogurt and White-Chocolate Cheesecake

Here's a new twist on cheesecake. A shortbread base hosts a cheesecake that is really more like a tart with its unusual yogurt instead of all cream cheese.

Base:
- 8 ounces shortbread (such as Carr's brand), finely crushed in a food processor
- 1/2 cup butter, melted

Filling:
- 8 ounces cream cheese
- 1/2 cup natural, plain, thick yogurt
- 1 tablespoon sugar
  Finely grated zest of and juice of 1 orange
- 10 ounces quality white chocolate, grated and melted
- 1 egg white

Topping:
- 1/2 cup grated, quality milk chocolate

continued on page 64

Rocky shores and glistening waters are the main ingredients for many a scenic vista in Connemara.

Sweet thoughts for a postcard to a friend: the unusual Yogurt and White-Chocolate Cheesecake at a Dutch marquetry desk in the parlor

Place the crushed shortbread in a mixing bowl and stir in the melted butter. Mix until smooth and transfer to the base of a 9-inch springform pan. Press the mixture over the bottom with the back of a spoon. Chill in the refrigerator for 30 minutes.

To make the filling, use a hand-held mixer to beat the cream cheese, yogurt, sugar, orange zest, and 2 tablespoons of the orange juice until smooth. Stir the melted chocolate into the cream cheese mixture until well incorporated. Set aside.

In another mixing bowl, whisk the egg white until stiff peaks form. Fold into the mixture until fully blended. Pour the mixture into the shortbread-lined pan and chill overnight. Next day, remove the cheesecake from the pan. Sprinkle with the grated chocolate. Keep chilled until ready to serve. Yield: 8 to 10 servings. ◆

Wine Suggestion

Sichel
Beerenauslese
Kirchheimer Römerstrasse

Estate Bottled by Paul Regenwiese, Kirchheim

The natural, rich, ripe-fruit sweetness of **Sichel Beerenauslese** comes from grapes that are carefully picked berry by berry, ensuring that only overripe grapes will be used to make this luscious dessert wine. It is excellent with this cheesecake or any flavorful cheese.

'...Out with the Scissors, Off to the Garden' for a Perfect Culinary Match

Chef Kevin Arundel

MARLFIELD HOUSE, WEXFORD

We asked this world-class chef if he would do one television show making three breakfast dishes and another show with appetizer, entree, and dessert. Most of the other chefs were preparing complete meals for two shows — two chances to show the world their talents.

We weren't sure how Kevin Arundel would react. After all, what's a chef to do to make breakfast exciting and reflective of his culinary prowess? Chef Arundel hid his disappointment and responded: "Yes, I can do that."

And in that five-word response lies the story, not only of this great young chef, but also of the place where he works. At Marlfield House, an 1820 sandstone Georgian treasure said to be the most-decorated country house hotel in Ireland, the only *can't* in the repertoire is this: They simply can't do enough for their guests.

You see it in the decor — lavishly appointed guest rooms that are larger than life. For example, there's the Print Room with its pen-and-ink sketches and *trompe l' oeil* painting on the walls, its massive 8-foot headboard, and a mahogany table double that length. You see it in the common rooms, where never is a guest wanting for a glass or a teacup. You see it in the gardens, where long ribbons of flowers and herbs are cared for like children in a nursery for newborns. And, best of all, you see it in the food here — five-course dinners that care enough about your palate not only to please it but to cleanse it as well with homemade sorbet.

Mary Bowe, owner and designer of Marlfield House, is the passion behind the magic at this country house hotel. Strutting peacocks about the grounds are her pets. And like each neatly formed feather on her birds, every detail at Marlfield fans out into perfect shape as a guest enters. Mary Bowe was *chef de cuisinaire* in the kitchen at Marlfield for more than a decade before she hired a chef. She understands what it takes to make for a gracious stay from stove to linen closet, and so do judges of the many culinary, gardening, and hospitality competitions that honor her place every year.

Kevin Arundel takes to heart the pampering and rapture that Mary Bowe wants her guests to experience at Marlfield. He aims to please. His menu changes nightly and is based on what's only minutes old. "At half-six in the evening, it's out with the scissors and off to the garden. So, if you called for a dinner reservation at 7:30, the lettuce put in your salad would only have been picked an hour earlier. The food has to suit the luxury of the house," says the chef.

Kevin suggests making your dinner match your own style: "Prepare what you like. Reflect

who you are or you won't do well. At Marlfield, we prepare what we like. No matter who is coming for dinner, we do what we do best." The "who" that comes for dinner includes a prestigious list of celebrities from rock stars and other musicians to ambassadors and presidents.

Born in County Cork in 1968, Chef Arundel typifies what's happening on the culinary scene in Ireland. In the last five years, he and many other young cooks left Ireland to study under the masters in France and elsewhere. "Now," he notes, "the Irish chefs are all coming back, bringing with them new ideas based on old-classic French style. It's very exciting." Well, we certainly can see that in Chef Arundel — even in his breakfast! (See pages 71-73 for the chef's early-morning recipes and the story of the Irish Breakfast.) ◆

Baked Chicken Breast with a Hazelnut Mousse and a Red Wine Sauce over Potato Rosti

Chef Arundel espouses the philosophy that red wine doesn't just go with red meat, and white with seafood and poultry. Here, he brings the red wine directly into the cooking of chicken. This dish bursts with flavor. You can depend on it to bring *oohs* and *aahs* from your dinner guests. You will find that it will become one of your trusty dinner-party recipes. The rosti, made of potato, forms the bed upon which the chicken sits, surrounded by the sauce.

The chicken with hazelnut mousse

Chicken:
4   boned chicken breasts
    Salt
¼   cup heavy cream
¼   cup clarified butter
2   tablespoons roasted, chopped hazelnuts

Sauce:

- ½ cup red wine
- 2 tablespoons port wine
- 1 tablespoon red wine vinegar
- 1 cup veal or beef stock
- 1 tablespoon butter
- 16 small shallots, peeled
- 10 small cloves garlic, peeled
- ½ cup clarified butter

Potato Rosti:

- 2 medium potatoes, peeled
-   Salt and pepper
-   Butter for frying

Garnish:

- 2 shallots
- 1 clove garlic
- 1 sprig fresh thyme

Remove the filets from the chicken breasts. In a blender, blend the filets with a sprinkling of salt for about 1 minute. Remove from the blender and fold in the cream and clarified butter. Check for seasoning and add more salt to taste. Fold in the nuts. Set aside. Slit each breast down the center, forming a pocket. Using a pastry bag (or a teaspoon will do), pipe in the hazelnut mousse. Secure each breast with at least three toothpicks to keep the mousse intact.

Cook the chicken breasts in a skillet with a little butter until the breasts have browned, adding more butter if necessary. Set aside in a glass baking dish.

Start the sauce by placing all of the sauce ingredients except the veal stock into a pan. Cook over medium-high heat until the liquid reduces to about half. Add the veal stock, and reduce by two-thirds. Pass through a sieve. Return to the pan and keep warm.

Meanwhile, make the potato rosti or pancakes. You can do this one of two ways. Either place small, single egg-size skillets on the stove or use one medium skillet to form the rosti. Shred the potato on the large-hole side of a hand grater. Season the potato with salt and pepper. Add a little butter to each pan and evenly spread the grated potato into each pan. The natural starch from the cooking potato and the butter will hold the potato together. Cook until crisp on both sides. Remove from pan and let drain on a paper towel. (Note: If using a larger skillet, cut the rosti into 4 equal parts.)

Place the peeled shallots and garlic in aluminum foil with the clarified butter. Bake in the oven at 350° for 20 minutes. Place the seared-and-stuffed chicken breasts into the oven for the last 7 to 8 minutes that shallots, garlic, and thyme are roasting. Remove from the oven and begin to assemble the dish. Slice the chicken breasts into ³/₄-inch slices.

Place the rosti in the center of the serving plate. Add the chicken on top. Surround with sauce and garnish with the shallots and garlic. Yield: 4 servings. ◆

Wine Suggestion

A handsome poultry dish like this one cries out for an elegant robust wine such as **Riserva Ducale** (The Duke's Reserve) from the *Tuscan Estates of Ruffino*. The Sangiovese grape provides a concentration of fruit and excellent structure for a truly classic pairing with the baked chicken breast.

The regal touch topping off the Georgian suite at Marlfield House is a carved wooden cornice, setting the backdrop for a chocolate marquise tart.

Dark Chocolate Marquise Tart in a Coffee Bean Sauce

Marquise:

3 ½   cups heavy cream
      Zest of 2 oranges
16   ounces sweet, quality dark chocolate
¼   cup butter
2   tablespoons brandy

Sauce:

1   cup milk
1   tablespoon coffee beans, ground
4   egg yolks
2   tablespoons sugar

Raspberry Purée:

1   cup fresh raspberries
2   tablespoons sugar
1   tablespoon water

Garnish:

    Fresh bunch mint leaves

In a medium saucepan, heat 2 cups of the cream and the orange zest. Bring to a boil and remove from the heat. Add the chocolate and blend until smooth. Add the butter and incorporate well.

In a separate bowl, whip the remaining cream and brandy together until soft peaks form. Fold into the chocolate mixture and pour into an 11 x 4 ½ x 2 ¾-inch loaf pan. Place in the refrigerator for 1 to 2 hours to mold.

Prepare the coffee sauce. Heat the milk with the ground coffee in a small saucepan over medium-high heat. Beat the egg yolks and sugar together in a mixing bowl. Pour the milk mixture into the egg mixture and then back into the saucepan. Cook until the mixture thickens over medium-high heat. Remove from heat and set aside until ready to use.

To make the raspberry purée, mix all the ingredients in a blender until smooth.

When the terrine is ready, cut ⅓-inch-thick slices and then cut across diagonally. Pool the coffee sauce onto a serving plate and add the marquise. Place a scoop of sorbet or ice cream onto the plate, if desired. Drop the raspberry purée from the tip of a teaspoon onto the sauce as pictured. Garnish with raspberry purée and mint. Yield: 12 servings. ◆

Wine Suggestion

The thickly textured **Sichel Trockenbeerenauslese** dessert wine marries well with the sumptuousness of the chocolate and cream, and the bright zesty tang of orange and raspberries in Chef Arundel's tart. Trockenbeerenauslese refers to the method of hand harvesting only dried (trocken) grapes that have been attacked by noble rot. At this stage, the grapes look more like berries (beeren), and are bursting with sweet, syrupy juice.

The harmony between fine food and elegant surroundings is perfected at Marlfield House. A plate of tortellini (see recipe in Pantry section on page 208) and the chef's chicken with hazelnut mousse in the gathering room

Top o' the Mornin' with Heart, Soul, and Bacon

What's in an Irish Breakfast?

Wherever you visit in Ireland, whether in a private home, a country house, bed-and-breakfast or luxury hotel, you will likely find the option of an Irish Breakfast on the menu first thing in the morning. When you see the phrase *Irish Breakfast,* it means full-meal ahead, consisting of a potpourri of early morning fare from the steaming-hot bowls of porridge, scones with homemade preserves, and fresh-picked fruit to the more savory of ingredients such as salmon pies, boxty (potato pancakes), rice puddings, and for the more adventurous, the black puddings (resembling sausage but made up of cooked animal blood, milk, seasonings, and usually oatmeal).

The Irish Breakfast was originally served at 10 a.m. after the farm chores were completed. Known as the *fry,* it included pork, potatoes, grains, dairy products, whisky, and ale.

There's always a heaping portion of sausages and the world's best breakfast ham — Irish bacon — plus pots of full-bodied teas and coffees.

As you can tell by now, there's nothing meek or mild about an Irish Breakfast. This is the time to fasten your culinary seat belt and dig in, beginning the day heartily.

There are no hard-and-fast rules as to what type of dishes comprise the traditional meal. But the underlying expectation seems always to be that it is served with great heart and soul — a spirited mix of hospitality — and always a handsome order of delicious Irish bacon as well as plenty of flavorful brown bread. Irish bacon is meatier and more like a ham than bacon in America. It is available in some places in this country. Ask your butcher or see page 217 under the Shannon Traditional listing to order.

Brown bread is the Irish staple bread or national loaf that has been around for centuries. There are many variations on the brown bread recipe throughout the Emerald Isle, but we found the one at Marlfield House to be at the top of the list. (See Chef Kevin Arundel's recipe on page 206.)

Each cook has his or her own interpretation of an Irish Breakfast. At Marlfield, Chef Arundel offered *World Class Cuisine* a few recipes, including pancakes made with beer, veal kidneys doused with brandy and wrapped in bacon, and eggs scrambled with mushrooms and haddock. Serve these with fresh fruits, cereals, and Kevin's brown bread.

Marlfield House also adds caramelized melon to the menu as well as toasted nuts and whisky porridge to mention a few choices.

"The Irish are serious about breakfast," comments Chef Arundel. In the Marlfield kitchen it takes two chefs and a staff of assistants to get the bacon to the table so to speak. Chef Arundel explains that an Irish Breakfast is a pampering thing. "We love being able to help people start the day with a full stomach and a lot of good cheer to set their mood." ◆

Smoked Haddock in a Brie-and-Chive Sauce with Scrambled-Egg Quenelles and Oyster Mushrooms

Seafood first thing in the morning offers great eye-opening taste, and this version by Chef Arundel is bound to please family and friends. Quenelles are primarily oval-shaped mounds, similar to dumplings but comprised of meats or seafood, bound with eggs. This recipe is fun to prepare and can even be served with a green salad for a quick dinner.

Haddock:
- 12 ounces smoked haddock
- 2 tablespoons butter, melted

Mushrooms:
- 1 tablespoon butter
- 1 shallot, finely diced
- 8 ounces oyster or button mushrooms, sliced

Sauce:
- 2 ounces Brie cheese, chopped
- 1/2 cup light or heavy cream
- 1 bunch fresh chives, chopped
- Salt and pepper

Eggs:
- 1 tablespoon butter for sautéing or no-stick cooking spray
- 4 eggs
- 2 tablespoons light or heavy cream
- Salt and pepper

Slice the haddock into thin slices. Place the fish in a skillet with the butter and cook gently over medium heat for about 3 or 4 minutes or just until heated through. Set aside and keep warm.

Prepare the mushrooms. In a small skillet, heat the butter and add the shallots. Cook for 1 minute. Add in the mushrooms and cook for 3 minutes more. Keep warm.

Make the sauce by placing the cheese in a small saucepan with the cream and the chives. Season with salt and pepper to taste and allow to warm on the stove over low heat (stirring occasionally), just enough for the cheese to melt, about 15 minutes. Keep warm.

In another skillet, melt the butter over medium-high heat. In a bowl, lightly beat the eggs and cream with a wire whisk. Season with salt and pepper. Pour the mixture into the heated skillet as the butter starts to sizzle. Scramble the eggs for 2 minutes or just enough to cook them to desired doneness.

Assemble by placing the haddock in the center of the plate. Pour on some of the cheese sauce. Add the mushrooms to the center of the plate. Top with some scrambled eggs, shaped as though a football or a quenelle, or just place the eggs on top of the mushrooms as desired. Finish the remaining 3 plates the same way. Yield: 4 servings. ◆

Pot o' Gold Pancakes with Cheese and Stout

Guinness, Ireland's national stout, is the gold in these pancakes. The drink is a dark beer with a creamy head that has a rich, distinct taste. Substitute with another stout, if necessary. You can serve these with honey or maple syrup, but Chef Arundel suggests melting some butter in a saucepan, adding a little sugar and lemon juice to taste, and warming the mixture until ready to serve.

- 1/2 cup all-purpose flour
- 2 tablespoons sugar
- 1/8 teaspoon salt
- 1 egg
- 1 egg yolk
- 1/2 cup milk
- 2 tablespoons butter, melted
- 2 tablespoons Guinness stout
- 2 ounces Edam cheese, finely grated
- Butter for frying

In a large mixing bowl, sift together the flour, sugar, and salt. Add the egg and the egg yolk and gradually stir in the milk, stirring constantly. Stir in the melted butter. Add the beer and beat well. The batter should be the consistency of thin cream. If too thick, add a little more beer. Add the cheese into the batter. Let the batter stand at room temperature for 30 minutes.

When ready to cook the pancakes, heat butter in a 6-inch, no-stick skillet and pour in 3 to 4 tablespoons of batter for each pancake. Cook the batter until the bottom is golden. Flip the pancake and cook on the other side. (Be cautious of burning as the cheese from the mixture may stick to the pan.) Repeat until all of the batter is used up. Serve as suggested or just hot with some butter. Yield: 4 to 6 thin pancakes. ◆

A bounteous Irish Breakfast is cordially served in the drawing room at Marlfield House. From left: the haddock and eggs, the brandied kidneys; and the pancakes. To make the kidneys, marinate 8 kidneys (or substitute with beef liver) in ¼ cup brandy for 6 hours. Wrap in bacon (Irish bacon preferred) and brush with melted butter. Grill until crisp. Serve with a fresh tomato filled with a country-style mustard. For the haddock and pancakes, see individual recipes.

Reflections of grandeur, the Palace Hotel, Bussaco

PORTUGAL

Cabo da Roca,
westernmost
point in all
Europe

Caldo Verde, the national dish

A Fairy Tale Comes True in an Enchanted Forest

Chef Manuel Lourenço

PALACE HOTEL BUSSACO, MEALHADA

Once upon a time in a land far from the sea, the city, and civilization, a king carved out a grand palace for the game-hunting season. He enshrined it with heavy granite and embedded it with large tile tableaus, telling of mythological and Medieval heroes and contemporary warriors. He added stained glass, sumptuous stairways and marble floors, and was attended by an army of servants and cooks.

Fairy tales do come true. You see, not much has changed since the last, long-term sire of Portugal, King Charles I, did build his splendid summer retreat at the turn of this century. Today, with a staff of devoted innkeepers and servers, there is no denying the royal fashion to which guests are treated here.

A twisting roadway paves the path to the palace, nestled amidst 250 acres of pristine timberland. From the moment a bellboy swings open the door, the hospitality is fervent and genuine. Guest rooms are individually decorated and the still of the night is everything you might imagine from a sleep in an emerald-green woodland.

Meals are served in the main dining room, overlooking an arched terrace and expansive gardens with a pond — home to two playful swans that flutter about at the far reaches of the gardens. Chef Manuel Lourenço presides among all the fantasy at Bussaco as he has for thirty years, extending his unwavering desire: "My only dream is to go on serving guests with the best there is," says the chef, who still "hears" the king's carriage and horses trotting up the hill.

The partridge, fit for a king (The wine bottled in the palace cellar is available only at Bussaco. The regal Baron de Chirel is recommended as the perfect accompaniment to the partridge. See recipe and wine suggestion on page 80.)

◆ CHEF MANUEL LOURENÇO ◆

At lunch and dinner, a four-course spread from a constantly changing menu greets guests, who are literally surrounded by history — wall motifs from the age of discovery painted in Manuelan fashion. The inlaid floor of oak and pine from the Bussaco forest mirrors the star pattern on the cassette-style ceiling, while hutches of chestnut grace the dining room, which has intricately carved moldings.

Antiques abound at the hotel, and they include the silverware, a French design in use since the 1930s. Every place setting includes a Neptune fork for the wonderful seafood Chef Lourenço prepares.

The wine cellar of the hotel is a magical place. A handful of hired helpers bottle and cork — by hand — the hotel's special red and white, which bear the proud Bussaco label. A bottle from the year of your birth probably still rests peacefully in the cool and tranquil cellar, collecting the dust of the ages.

Perhaps what this very special place embodies is all in the words of Chef Lourenço: "Indoors and outdoors, this is a fascinating place: the forest all around; the garden nursings; the landscape; the waterfalls fresh and clear from the hills. You can feel nature and its blessings." ◆

Chickpea and Spinach Soup

Typically, chickpeas are a favorite ingredient in recipes from most Mediterranean countries. Portugal is no exception. This hearty soup is delicious and very easy to prepare.

1 cup dried chickpeas
1 onion, diced
3 ½ ounces uncooked bacon strips
3 ½ ounces chorizo or other garlic-style sausage, chopped
2 tablespoons olive oil
Salt
4 cups fresh spinach, washed and coarsely chopped

Soak the chickpeas in water overnight. Add them to a large saucepan, covering the peas with about 3 pints of water. Add the onion, bacon, sausage, and oil. Season with salt to taste. Bring the mixture to a boil over high heat. Turn the heat down and allow the soup to cook gently until peas are well done, about 2 hours. Remove peas and meats from the broth and skim the fat. Transfer the mixture to a food processor and purée until smooth. Return to the pan. Turn the heat up to a boil and drop in the spinach, boiling over medium-high heat for just 5 minutes or until the spinach is just cooked tender. Serve hot. Yield: 6-8 servings. ◆

Wine Suggestion

The **Marqués de Riscal Rueda** from neighboring Spain is a dry, crisp, and medium-bodied white wine that makes a flavorful accompaniment to hearty Mediterranean dishes like the chickpea soup.

Rueda is the name of the beautiful and romantic region that gave birth to this, one of Marqués de Riscal's classic, dry white wines. Its liveliness makes it an excellent choice for those dishes containing a variety of ingredients and tastes.

Chickpea and Spinach Soup on the terrace at the Palace Hotel

Stuffed Bussaco Partridge on Liver Toast with White Asparagus

Not too far from the palace hotel is a pheasant farm where fresh poultry is selected for the chef's kitchen. Partridge is a favorite dish at the hotel (see photo page 77). This version is stuffed with a liver pâté of your choice and requires a 24-hour marinating time.

4	slices crusty stale bread, finely crumbled, or 2 cups breadcrumbs
1 $^1/_2$	cups liver pâté of choice
1	cup sunflower oil
$^1/_2$	cup diced sweet (gherkins-style) pickles
4	partridge, cleaned, or small Cornish hens
3 $^1/_2$	cups ruby port wine
3 $^1/_2$	cups white wine
	Salt and pepper
4	slices whole-wheat bread, crusts removed
12	white asparagus spears, cooked

In a small bowl, mix together the breadcrumbs, 1 cup of the pâté, the oil, and the pickles. Evenly divide the stuffing and spoon into each partridge cavity.

Using kitchen string, tie the legs of the partridge to hold in the stuffing. Place partridges in a Dutch oven and fill this pan with the port and white wines. Season with salt and pepper. Allow to sit in the refrigerator to marinate for 24 hours, turning birds frequently.

About 2 hours before serving time, cook the partridges over medium heat in the Dutch oven and cook for at least 1$^1/_2$ hours with the lid on the pan or until birds are cooked through. Remove the partridges from the pan. Remove the thread. Set aside and keep warm. Return the Dutch oven to the heat, cooking the wine sauce until it is reduced by half.

Meanwhile, toast the bread and spread it with the remaining liver pâté. Place a piece of toast on each serving plate. Add a partridge and pour wine sauce over each plate. Add white asparagus spears (warmed) and serve. Yield: 4 servings. ◆

Wine Suggestion

A meal fit for a king at a palace like Bussaco deserves a regal wine, **Baron de Chirel,** from the Rioja region of Spain. The deep, rich, and complex Reserva is the perfect accompaniment to a multi-faceted dish like the partridge. This wine is made 70 percent from Cabernet grapes and 30 percent from the indigenous Tempranillo grape variety.

> 66
>
> *Indoors and outdoors, this is a fascinating place: the forest all around; the garden nursings; the landscape; the waterfalls fresh and clear from the hills. You can feel nature and its blessings.*
>
> 99

CHEF MANUEL LOURENÇO

Exploring Culinary Riches in a New Age of Discovery

Chef Helmut Ziebell

HOTEL RITZ, LISBON

Five-hundred years ago, Portuguese navigators departed from the Tagus River in old Lisbon to unlock the secrets of new worlds. Today, a proud chef offers his guests the treasures of a time long ago as his city pulses around him in direct contrast: Skyscrapers in Lisbon dwarf old fish markets where passersby watch the ancient custom of scaling and selling the day's catch. Winding, cobblestone roads to the city's seven hills host worshippers who find the solace of each mount reason enough to pause, pray the rosary, and watch the activities of the river.

It is little wonder that Austrian-born Chef Helmut Ziebell deigns to promote Portugal, a country that played an integral role in the age of discovery. The country's history is a part of the chef's environment at the Hotel Ritz.

The hotel resonates with Old World charm: museum-quality paintings, tapestries, and sculptures abound, telling their stories of Portugal's swashbuckling past and its golden era of riches brought about by the brave explorations of the fifteenth and sixteenth centuries. The Verandah dining room is filled with this art and some period pieces. Flanking the entryway to the restaurant are two silver, antique duck presses that once squeezed the juice from poultry bones for sauce. Marble graces sideboards and crafted mahogany forms built-ins and columns. Velvet upholstery on eighty wood-framed chairs is replaced every year and damask tablecloths shimmer in the sun at breakfast and in candlelight at dinner.

Matching all of this world-class ambiance is a fitting menu by Chef Ziebell, who cooks Portuguese with an international flair. From salmon grilled as soft as silk to veal medallions rich in a savory sauce, the cuisine of this chef is some of the best in all of Portugal.

Although he prepared strictly traditional dishes for *World Class Cuisine,* he has his own cooking philosophy. With a twinkle in his eyes as blue and deep as traditional Portuguese *azulejo* tiles, this chef — who once wanted to be an artist but realized it was food that could earn him a living — explains: "A young painter told his master, Degas, that he had finally found his painting style. Degas responded, 'How boring.' But if I *have to* speak about my style," the chef notes, "I would say my cooking is the art of combining the traditional with the new."

Chef Ziebell pads intently around his large kitchen at the Ritz in a pair of white clogs. Many members of his staff of forty follow him in his footwear as well as his cooking style. Food by Chef Ziebell is intense and robust with the unmistakable look and taste of fourteen-carat elegance.

Although his roots are elsewhere, the chef's heart is in Portugal where he has lived for nearly three decades with his Portuguese wife, Maria, and their three children. ◆

Beef Portuguesa with Honey-Vegetable Sauce and Potatoes

Hearty, but offering a delicate, memorable flavor, this aromatic dish is great served with a crusty bread for dipping in the flavorful brown sauce. You will be making the sauce first. Be sure to thin the sauce with a little water, if necessary. Add more honey for a sweeter sauce.

Sauce:

6	medium garlic cloves, crushed
1	tablespoon olive oil
1 1/2	cups white wine
1	tablespoon vinegar
6	black peppercorns, crushed
6	small laurel or bay leaves
1 1/2	cups brown veal stock (or other brown stock)
3	tablespoons ketchup
1	teaspoon honey
1	small carrot, chopped
1	small onion, chopped
1	small ginger root, diced
1	cup sliced leek (white part only), diced
1/4	cup celery, chopped

In a medium saucepan, sauté the garlic in olive oil until translucent. Add the wine and vinegar to the pan and stir. Add the pepper, bay leaves, veal stock, ketchup, and honey. Stir well. Add the remaining vegetables and bring the mixture to a boil. Cook over medium-high heat until the sauce is reduced by half or at desired consistency. Pass the sauce through a sieve and keep warm.

Beef:

4	large white potatoes
1/4	cup olive or vegetable oil or more to sauté Salt and pepper
4	beef tenderloin steaks (about 1/2 pound each)
1	tablespoon butter or cholesterol-free margarine
4	cloves garlic
4	laurel or bay leaves
4	slices prosciutto (soak ham in water for a few minutes or longer to remove excess salt) Chopped parsley for garnish

Peel the potatoes. In a medium saucepan, boil the potatoes until *al dente* (not soft). Drain and cut the potatoes into 1/4-inch slices. In a large skillet, heat the oil and sauté the potatoes over medium heat until they are slightly browned but not crisp. Season with salt and pepper. Remove from the pan with a

continued on page 84

A tapestry devoted to Lisbon's golden age of discovery forms the backdrop for Beef Portuguesa.

slotted spoon onto a paper towel. Set aside and keep warm, returning the pan to the heat.

Add more oil to the pan (just enough to sauté), if necessary. Season the steaks on both sides with salt and pepper. Cook the steaks in the pan over medium-high heat, turning on both sides to obtain a medium-rare inside. Remove from heat and keep warm. Preheat the oven to 350°.

Butter a 9x13-inch glass baking dish. Crush the garlic cloves and place them around the dish. Add the bay leaves in the center of the dish, so that each steak will fit over a leaf. Place the steaks over the leaves and scatter the potatoes all around. Top with the sauce.

Bake in the oven until the sauce begins to boil (about ½ hour). Serve in individual dishes with a slice of ham on each steak and a sprinkling of chopped parsley. Add extra sauce. Discard the bay leaves. Yield: 4 servings. ◆

Wine Suggestion

The rich and savory beef marries well with the concentrated and beautifully balanced **Rioja Reserva,** from Marqués de Riscal, leader in the production of Rioja wine since the early nineteenth century. The combination of rich, berry character and earthiness helps bring together the veritable artist's palette of flavors found in this scintillating beef dish.

Fresh Orange Roll with Raspberry Sauce

Easy to prepare, this dessert makes you look like a culinary expert. The Portuguese serve this with thread-like ovos or egg strings as a garnish (see photo), made by pouring eggs through a strainer and into boiling water. Here, however, you simply prepare the orange roll with raspberry sauce made by puréeing fresh raspberries and sugar to taste, and adding a fresh sprig of mint.

6	eggs
¾	cup sugar plus more for sprinkling
1 ½	tablespoons cornstarch
1	cup orange juice
	Grated peel of 1 orange
	Butter or non-stick spray
2	tablespoons cinnamon/sugar mixture
	Raspberry sauce
	Fresh mint for garnish

Columbus looks to the New World from atop Lisbon's Monument to the Discoveries.

This antique azulejo tile makes a splendid host for the orange roll.

Preheat the oven to 325°. Break the eggs into a bowl and mix them with ³/4 cup sugar. (Do not beat.) In a medium-size bowl, dissolve the cornstarch in the orange juice. Add the egg-and-sugar mixture and then the orange peel.

Prepare the pan. Grease a 9x13-inch jellyroll pan with butter. Sprinkle with sugar. Pour the egg-and-orange mixture into the prepared pan. Bake for 20 minutes or until a rich golden color. (Roll will be moist inside but cooked.)

Prepare a damp cloth or tea towel with the cinnamon/sugar mixture. Carefully remove roll from the pan, turning it out onto the cloth. Roll up, using the cloth as a pusher. Slice into ¹/2 to ³/4-inch slices. Add a pool of raspberry sauce to each individual serving plate. Place 2 to 4 pieces onto the sauce. Garnish with mint. Yield: 4-6 servings. ◆

Wine Suggestion

Sichel Eiswein
Flonheimer Adelberg

Estate Bottled by Wilfried Wiener, D- 6509 Flonheim

Unctuous, sweet, and full of ultra-ripe fruit flavors, the **Sichel Eiswein** is a wonderful match with desserts calling for fresh fruit and fruit purée.

A Castle in the Clouds Courts Royal Cuisine
Chef Fernando Piña Afonso

POUSADA DA RAINHA SANTA ISABEL, ESTREMOZ

*T*he beatified Queen Isabel, wife of King Dinis, devoted her life to the poor during the 14th century, much to the chagrin of the king. One day, she was stopped by the king as she was leaving the castle with bread for the sick and the poor. Suspecting that she was disobeying his orders, the king asked her to show him what she was carrying. As she opened her apron, the bread she had been holding turned to roses.

Such is the legend that pervades the great halls and palatial chambers of the Santa Isabel. Today, the king and queen's former residence contains thirty-three guest rooms and a stone-vaulted dining room complete with one-hundred sixty throne-like chairs of red velvet and brass tacks. The Santa Isabel is a pousada, a word derived from the Portuguese *pousar,* meaning rest and welcome. The pousadas are restored historic buildings — from monasteries to castles to large estates. Owned by the government and run by private enterprise, pousadas are this country's way of saving old buildings and fostering Portuguese culture.

The Santa Isabel is one of the country's most elegant and famous pousadas. And, like all of the pousadas, one of its missions is to keep alive the regional and traditional cuisine of Portugal. That is Chef Fernando Piña Afonso's job, as it has been for twenty-three years except for a short, honorary stint in Paris where he was the chef at a Portuguese restaurant. He was educated primarily through the pousada system, which includes an impressive program for continuing culinary education. When not cooking, he may be found fishing for the catch that will end up on his grill.

"What I like most about my job," offers the chef, "is to serve regional food." For Chef Afonso, that means Alentejan cooking, earmarked by such foods as lamb stews, game meats, and sweets made with lots of eggs. Portugal introduced the world to the refinements of sugar and began incorporating it with eggs, creating our first desserts. Often just the egg yolks were used in such preparations because the nuns (who gave Portugal many of its famous dessert recipes) needed egg whites to starch their habits. The *Bolo de Convento* or Convent Cake offered here is very typical of Portuguese sweets.

Meals at the pousada could fill a king's army. In fact, Portugal is known for its large portions. At the Santa Isabel, meals are presented on china plates with silver chargers etched with the castle's original crest. Ornate wall sconces and five-foot-tall chandeliers are made with carved wood, as are scrolled cornices that yield to flowing velvet drapes. For a night at the pousada, you are given the keys to the kingdom with all its riches — culinary and otherwise. ◆

Daybreak, and Queen Isabel still watches over the square outside the castle.

Mini Chicken-and-Sausage Pies

In Portugal, they call chickens hens and thus this recipe is usually called *empadas de galinha* or hen pies. Easy to prepare, these make great hors d'oeuvres or lunch pies with a fresh garden salad.

Filling:
- 1 small chicken, giblets removed
- 1/4 cup vinegar
- 2 tablespoons olive oil
- 2 cups water
- 1/2 cup white wine
- 1 large onion
- 2 cloves garlic
- 1 teaspoon sea salt
- 1 sprig parsley, chopped
- 1 sprig marjoram, chopped, or 1/2 teaspoon dried
- 1 medium chorizo or other garlic-style sausage (about 1/2 to 1 pound), cut into 1/4-inch slices, Skimmed fat from cooled broth or butter

Pastry:
- 2 cups all-purpose flour
- 2 eggs
- Up to 1/2 cup skimmed fat from the broth or butter
- 1 egg beaten for egg wash

Fill a large saucepan with all of the filling ingredients except the sausage. Cook over medium to medium-high heat until the chicken begins to come away from the bone, about 40 to 50 minutes. When the meat is cooked, remove from the pan with a slotted spoon and cut or break into small pieces. Reserve the broth, strain it, and place in the refrigerator or freezer to cool.

When the broth has chilled and fat forms, preheat the oven to 350°. Prepare the pastry. Sift the flour into a large mixing bowl, add the 2 eggs and knead by hand, adding any fat that has collected on the surface of the chilled broth (or add softened butter by the tablespoonful as needed to make the dough pliable). Knead until the dough is soft but not sticky. Roll the pastry out to 1/4-inch thickness. Line

continued on page 89

Mini Chicken-and-Sausage Pies are dwarfed by the castle's tower.

12 pastry or cupcake tins with the dough. Stamp out 2-inch rounds for the tops of the pies.

Fill each cup with the chicken, a spoonful of the broth, and 1 or 2 pieces of the sausage. Cover with a circle of pastry. Seal the bottom of the pie to the top with the egg wash. Bake for 20 to 30 minutes, checking for doneness. Pies will be golden brown. Yield: 12 pies. ◆

3 tablespoons all-purpose flour
6 egg yolks
4 egg whites
1 teaspoon powdered yeast
1 teaspoon cinnamon

Glaze:
1 cup powdered sugar
1 tablespoon lemon juice
1 teaspoon walnut or vegetable oil
1 tablespoon water

Use a candy thermometer and heat the water with the sugar to boiling. Remove from the heat. Mix in the almonds, butter, egg yolks, and cinnamon. Return the mixture to the stove and cook until it thickens slightly, about 3 to 4 minutes. Remove from the heat and mix in the crystallized fruits.

Transfer the mixture into a large bowl and beat with electric mixer just until incorporated, about 1 minute. Allow to cool. Mix in the flour and the yeast. Set aside. In another bowl, beat the egg whites until stiff peaks form. Fold into the fruit mixture.

Grease a 9-inch springform pan and bake at 350° for 15 minutes or until tester inserted comes clean. Allow cake to cool to lukewarm.

Prepare the glaze. Mix together all the glaze ingredients and spread evenly on lukewarm cake. Yield: 10-12 servings. ◆

Wine Suggestion

The chicken and chorizo sausage, especially when combined with herbs and spices, need the strength of a full-bodied Rioja. The Tempranillo grape produces flavors of red berries and mushrooms in the **Marqués de Riscal Rioja Reserva.**

Convent Cake

Simple and full of fruit flavor, this moist cake, first invented by nuns who made great use of eggs, is easy to prepare and delicious.

Cake:
2 tablespoons water
1 cup sugar
1 cup ground almonds
3 tablespoons butter
1/4 cup each and chopped crystallized: pumpkin, cherries, and orange peels

Wine Suggestion

Only specially selected, late-harvested berries are used to make **Sichel Beerenauslese,** a delicate dessert wine that marries perfectly with fresh fruit or a simple cake such as Chef Afonso's.

The delicious Convent Cake stands guard over Estremoz.

Regional Culinary Adventure Just Under the Stars

Chef Maria da Conceição Lourenço

POUSADA DE SANTA MARIA, MARVÃO

arväo. Say the name to the Portuguese and a look of peace follows on their faces. This village of three hundred, that reaches for the sky from a mountaintop overlooking the Spanish border, is a very special place.

Tucked far into the Iberian outback, Marvão is made up of narrow, cobblestone streets where the houses are white-washed and the terra-cotta tiles of the roofs provide contrast. Protected by a scalloped stone wall, the village highlights include a church, a magnificent castle, and one of the country's most charming dining rooms at the Pousada de Santa Maria.

Chef Conceição Lourenço is the cook at the helm of a small staff that hosts as many as eighty diners in an evening. The food is very special at this former estate. It is prepared ever so carefully and proudly by a chef whose cooking stems humbly from the school of hands-on. She spent years growing up in the kitchen and learning Portuguese cooking before picking up professional techniques.

Chef Conceição's time has come. The world is looking for fine, ethnic/regional cooking, and has found it in a big way at the Santa Maria. The chef explains: "My cooking is regional but imaginative — using ingredients of the land mixed with tasteful seasonings. In the Alentejo region, almost everyone lives on agriculture. People from all over the world eat in our dining room, and the best we can give them is a part of our land and ourselves."

The food brought up from the kitchen makes its way to a cozy dining room where every table has a view through picture windows to a quilt of farmland with pockets of slightly larger towns than Marvão, and Spain in the distance.

Dinner always begins with locally grown olives and homemade bread. Soups, such as the one here made of garlic and coriander, are among the items on the menu that change according to seasonal ingredients. Chef Lourenço's seafood ranges from sea bass to red mullet, cooked to perfection.

A granite fireplace beams a golden glow into the dining room. Hand-painted pottery hangs about the restaurant, adding color to the pristine, white cotton-covered tables and the rush-seat, country ladderback chairs. Guests can take a cocktail or after-dinner drink in a quiet, low-ceilinged parlor where another fire burns slowly.

Desserts are important to the Portuguese, and at this pousada the staff wheels a mahogany cart-full — fresh from the pousada's ovens to your table. It is hard to choose.

A night at the Santa Maria — with its tastefully decorated country guest rooms, sporting designer fabrics in cheerful patterns and colors — is the cap to an enchanting evening in Chef Lourenço's dining room. When the sun sets and the moon rises, you too will feel you can reach out and touch a nearby star. ◆

Dusk falls on the Alentejo region.

Alentejan garlic soup in a Santa Maria parlor

Santa Maria Bread-and-Garlic Soup

Açorda à Alentejana is the Portuguese name for this soup. When you see the word *açorda* in a soup from this country, you know that it is a porridge-like broth, thickened with bread — very crusty bread made in brick or outdoor stone ovens. But any crusty, thick bread will do here. The eggs are optional but very much in the pousada's style.

---

1   large bunch (about 2 ½ cups) fresh coriander or pennyroyal or a mixture of both herbs, plus more for garnish
6   large cloves garlic, quartered
1   tablespoon coarse salt
4   eggs
¼   cup extra virgin olive oil
1 ½   quarts boiling water or chicken stock
¾   pound day-old crusty homemade bread, cut into 1 ½-inch chunks

---

Using a mortar and pestle, grind together the coriander, garlic, and salt until they form a paste. Turn the paste out into a large ovenproof bowl that can serve later as a tureen.

Poach the eggs in the boiling water for about 2 minutes. Remove carefully with a slotted spoon onto a flat plate or paper towel. Continue to boil the water slowly in the saucepan. Pour the olive oil over the paste in the baking dish. Add the boiling water from the poached eggs. Add the bread to the broth and place the poached eggs on top of the bread. When you are ready to serve, ladle the soup carefully, giving each individual bowl, bread and a poached egg. Sprinkle with more coriander for garnish, if desired. Yield: 4-6 servings. ◆

Baked Bream with Potatoes Alentejo Style

The olive oil, garlic, and tomatoes used as a base for dishes are a large part of the diet for the people of the Alentejo region of Portugal. This version of bream, a fish that hails back to Medieval times, yields a tender dish with a robust flavor.

½   cup olive oil
2   large onions, thinly sliced
2   pounds bream, red snapper, or orange roughy
2   cloves garlic, finely chopped
3   medium tomatoes, peeled and seeded
1   teaspoon paprika, plus more for sprinkling
1   tablespoon margarine
2   tablespoons chopped parsley
    Salt and freshly ground pepper
2   tablespoons butter, cut into four small pats
6   medium potatoes, peeled and sliced into ¼-inch medallions
½   cup white wine

Preheat the oven to 350°. Place the olive oil in a 9x13-inch baking dish. Add the onions, covering the bottom of the dish. Prepare the bream. Make 4 deep slits diagonally along the side of the fish. Place on top of the onions in the baking pan.

In a deep bowl, mix together the garlic, tomatoes, paprika, margarine, parsley, and salt and pepper to taste. Smash the ingredients together with the bottom of fork, mixing and forming the vegetables into a paste-like mixture. Rub the mixture into the slits of the fish and the outside. Add a pat of butter to the mixture inside each of the slits, if desired.

Sprinkle the potatoes lightly with salt, if desired, and paprika. Place around the fish in the baking dish. Bake the fish and potatoes in the oven for 25 to 30 minutes, or until potatoes are tender and fish is cooked through. Frequently baste the potatoes and the fish with liquid from the pan juices and the white wine. Yield: 6 servings. ◆

Wine Suggestion

NET CONTENTS
750 mL

ALCOHOL 12%
BY VOLUME

CHANDON
Carneros
Blanc de Noirs

CARNEROS SPARKLING WINE

The **Chandon Carneros Blanc de Noirs'** superb Pinot Noir and Pinot Meunier grapes from the cool Carneros district of California combine to produce a sparkling wine with the necessary fruit complexity and structure to complement the seasonings as well as the fish.

Fresh bream and ingredients for a superb recipe (You may also substitute with red snapper.)

Of Jigsaw-Puzzle Hillscapes and Port Wine

Chef Armando Paulino

LE MERIDIEN HOTEL, PORTO

Broken azulejo tiles are caught up with the seaweed and sand along the quay in picturesque old Porto. On the city side of the River Douro, hillside homes, with their cut-out shapes and traditional blue tiles sculpting doorways and windows, form a joyous jigsaw puzzle. In a suburb called Vila Nova da Gaia just across the river to the south, wine cellars filled with oak casks bearing such renowned names as *Sandeman* hold visitors spellbound. Some of the old barrels are two-stories tall. For this is the city that has given the world that most poetic of all drinks — port wine.

"Welcome to Porto," is the salute as the staff greets guests at the registration desk here at Le Meridien. A welcome tray holds small wine goblets, filled with ruby red port and glistening like gems — one for each guest.

Porto's roots can be seen on the river, where reproductions of ancient Phoenician, flat-bottomed boats still bounce and sway. These craft once carried barrels of grapes from the vineyards that lie up river. Porto's roots can also be seen at Balhao market, an open-air bazaar filled by bins cascading with colorful fruit, bounteous bouquets of bulbous garlic, terra-cotta bowls of native olives, squawking hens, and mountains of fresh, sea-drenched clams.

This is where Chef Armando Paulino shops to satisfy his thirst for the freshest ingredients. The farm and seafaring life come to the center of the bustling city at Balhao. Vendors keep warm, rubbing cold hands over tiny wood-burning grills. Some build up their own heat by moving about, shredding kale on a grinding wheel, or primping bright produce and voluptuous fruits.

Amid this festive mood, Chef Paulino browses, inspecting purchases with the care of a parent choosing ingredients for a new nursery. It is this kind of attention to detail that has helped earn him a Michelin star. Food is prepared by the chef with great style and flavor in a garden-style restaurant decorated with miles of peek-a-boo lattice.

French and continental dishes pervade the chef's menu as do traditional Portuguese favorites. The chef's cooking is heavily influenced by his hometown in the Algarve, the southernmost region of the country, where shellfish are abundant.

Chef Paulino received his culinary training in Switzerland and Egypt. "Don't try to disguise ingredients using heavy sauce," he reminds. The chef believes his success in the kitchen has to do with his being a "naturalist" all the way.

Enhancing the chef's fresh and elegant preparations is the elaborate decanting of port wine here. Sommelier Amaro Carvalho ceremoniously opens older bottles of port with fiery hot tongs tableside so that no grains from the cork — that has been soaking for years — are poured into a glass. (See more on port wine on page 101.) And so, the refined hospitality of Le Meridien, from front desk to the chef's kitchen, comes full circle at the dinner table. ◆

A vendor offers her garlic with pride at Balhao market.

Caldo Verde Soup

Probably no other dish more identifies this humble country than *caldo verde* or green soup (see photo page 75) made with cabbage-like greens and potatoes. Portuguese home cooks can even buy the kale freshly shredded at any one of the country's numerous fresh markets. Kale is rich in vitamins A and C.

Cabbage for the Caldo Verde is still shredded the old-fashioned way at Balhao market.

½   pound kale or collard greens, washed
3   tablespoons olive oil
4   ounces chorizo sausage, pepperoni, or any other garlic-seasoned, smoked pork sausage, cut into ¼-inch slices
1   large clove garlic, chopped
1   medium onion, diced
4   medium red potatoes, peeled
6   cups water
½   teaspoon freshly ground black pepper
    Salt to taste

Strip the kale leaves from the stem, bunching them together. With a very sharp knife, shred them into string-like threads. Set aside.

Place the oil, sausage, garlic, and onions in a small skillet. Sauté until lightly browned. Set aside.

In a medium saucepan, cook the potatoes in the water until they are soft enough to mash. Using a slotted spoon, transfer the potatoes to a bowl (leaving the water in the pan) and mash them with a fork until a smooth purée forms. Return the potatoes to the water in the saucepan. Stir in the pepper and salt, and bring to a boil over high heat. Add the kale and boil for 3 to 4 minutes more. Drop in the sausage, garlic, and onions and simmer for a couple of minutes to heat through. Serve. Yield: 6 servings. ◆

Wine Suggestion

The dry and somewhat smoky **Marqués de Riscal Sauvignon Blanc** is a refreshing and flavorful accompaniment to hearty Mediterranean dishes, including those such as Caldo Verde that contain herbs, spices, and hot pepper flavors. Made 100 percent from Sauvignon Blanc grapes, it's a superb match with fish and shellfish, too.

Pears in Port Wine Sauce

Pears draped with rich, ruby port make this an elegant and easy dessert to serve guests at home. As you might imagine, port is an integral cooking ingredient in this chef's kitchen. Choose pears that are fragrant and free of blemishes. Mother Nature protects pears by making them better to pick while still hard. Allow pears to ripen at room temperature.

---

4   cups quality ruby port wine
    Juice and peel of 2 lemons
1   cup sugar
2   cinnamon sticks, broken into pieces
8   medium pears (preferably Bosc or Anjou), peeled with stems left intact
    Water
    Whipping cream
    Fresh mint

In a large bowl, mix together the wine, lemon juice, lemon peel, sugar, and cinnamon sticks. In a large saucepan, add the pears and enough water to cover the pears. Boil the pears over medium-high heat for 15 minutes or until they are tender when pierced. (Cooking times will vary depending on the hardness and variety of the pears.)

Remove the pears from the saucepan with a slotted spoon. Set aside. Return the ruby port sauce to medium-high heat, cooking until it reduces to half and the liquid becomes syrupy. Discard the cinnamon pieces.

Cut the pears into quarters and in half again, carefully, removing and discarding the core. Fan out on a plate and add a pool of port sauce. Garnish with a dollop of whipped cream and a branch of fresh mint. Yield: 4 servings. ◆

Wine Suggestion

A luscious dessert wine made from dried, overripe berries, the **Sichel Trockenbeerenauslese** displays a harmony of complex, balanced flavors complementary to fresh fruit, sweet fruit desserts, or cheese.

Just outside Porto, the rural countryside is home to rustic farms, tiny villages, and port wine vineyards.

The dainty and elegant Pears in Port Wine Sauce (While port is the key ingredient in this sauce, Sichel's dessert wine also complements the fruit flavor of this dish. See recipe and wine suggestion on page 99.)

Sails in the Wind and the Man in the Black Cape
The Romance of Port Wine

*E*ver since I was a little girl, I have had a relationship with port wine. My father had a home bar, and I loved gazing at all of the advertising signs and memorabilia he had on display. One such collectible was a black figurine of a man in a sombrero and a long, flowing cape. The mysterious man always captured my curiosity.

My father used the product's name in his favor as a play on words. He would say, "That's the sandman and you know what that means — it's time for you to go to bed, young lady." I accepted his tale. The sandman sprinkled grains in our eyes to help us fall asleep. But the old cajoling ruse eventually wore off, and I got to the bottom of the black silhouette.

I became a lover of port wine both as an apéritif and for use in my cooking when I grew up. But it was not until my trip to Portugal for *World Class Cuisine* years later that I uncovered the real secrets of the man in the black cape and the story of port wine.

I learned that the silhouette has been a symbol for port wine, and that it came from the Sandeman company (actually pronounced sand-eh-man), maker of port and sherry since 1790. The "don," as the symbol has been called, is on all of the labels of spirits (now distributed by Seagrams) that the company bottles. Down by the River Douro in Porto there is a section called the Vila Nova da Gaia, and that is where

Sommelier Amaro Carvalho performs the intricate ceremony of decanting the port wine.

the mystery of the *sandeman* unfolds. Just beyond the river's edge, a flat-bottomed boat, carrying oak casks, a billowing canvas sail, and a life-size figure of the lone caballero, bobs, beckoning in the Portuguese breeze. On the river bank is his home — the Sandeman bodega or cave where harvested port ages in giant casks. Countless cellars of other port wine makers line the river next to Sandeman.

Vila Nova da Gaia is the world's home of port wine. While most of the harvesting is done three hours up river, this is where port is blended and rests before it is bottled and distributed all over the world. True port wine is produced with grapes from the Douro region, which consists of fifteen-thousand square miles of terraced vineyards with thousands of small and individual harvesters, supplying the big port makers.

> **66**
>
> *We care about the port wine like we care about the child.*
>
> **99**
>
> AMARO CARVALHO

Port comes in several styles, the most common of which are ruby, tawny, white, and vintage. The latter is the most expensive and best used as an apéritif while the others are for cooking as well as drinking. There is nothing like a glass of port, especially when the air chills and there is a fire blazing inside. Perhaps that is why port is also considered such a graceful and romantic drink. It is a prelude to yet a still young evening ahead.

Port may be served chilled, but sommelier Amaro Carvalho from the Hotel Meridien, suggests serving it at room temperature and leaving enough room in the glass for swirling. The wine should be served by the host, with the guest on his or her immediate left receiving the first glass.

Cheese is a notable accompaniment to port wine, especially hard cheeses. Port is a fortified wine and a strong cheese complements its fruitiness. Blue Stilton is said to be the best cheese with port. Cheddar and Monterey Jack are only two of the other possibilities. David Sandeman, chairman of the House of Sandeman (a family-run business for more than two-hundred years), adds that if you are enjoying several cheeses with port, mild cheeses should be served first and the more flavorful last.

Similar to other wines, port is made from fermented grapes. But just before the fermentation is complete and all of the grape sugar has been converted to alcohol, a neutral wine brandy is added to preserve some of the natural sweetness of the grapes.

The young port remains in vats until spring when it is shipped down river to Vila Nova da Gaia where cellarmasters watch over it as it matures. "We care about the port wine like we care about the child. It's very delicate," an insightful Amaro Carvalho tells *World Class Cuisine.*

The words ring true, somewhat like my father cared about me as he sent me off to bed many years ago, knowing the "sandeman" would always be with me. (For recipes using port, see index.) ◆

Port wine makes a delicious vinegar for sauces, salads and cooking. These recipes are from another port maker, the House of Croft.

Port Wine Vinegar:
Blend 1 part tawny port to 2 parts quality wine vinegar and let it rest for 6 months. Use as needed but keep in a container with a tight-fitting lid.

Red Meat Sauce: Mix together 2 tablespoons butter, $1/4$ cup ruby port; 1 tablespoon each worcestershire sauce and Dijon-style mustard. Heat to serve. ◆

Port wine vineyards and quintas - the original homes of vineyard landlords - dot the Douro River Valley outside Porto.

Neidpath Castle in Peebles

David Hunt prepares hot apple tarts.

SCOTLAND

The Scottish Queen of Puddings from Gleneagles

The Fabric of the River Tweed Is Woven in the Menu

Chef Ralph Brooks

EDNAM HOUSE HOTEL, KELSO

Scottish poet Sir Walter Scott, whose sage writings are immortalized wherever you go in this region, observed sometime in 1830: "Every valley has its battle and every stream its song." At Ednam House, the "good fight" to put fine food on the table every night persists for Chef Ralph Brooks in the kitchen as the song of the River Tweed flows past the small hotel.

"I grew up here, then went away and came back, realizing that this is as good as it gets," verbalizes the chef in his own lyrical way. Ednam House has been owned and operated by his mother and father for more than two decades. As a young boy, Ralph helped out at the hotel, doing an assortment of odd jobs everywhere except the kitchen. Then one day, every hand was needed in the cook's room, and Ralph was sent along to help. "To my surprise, I felt comfortable there," he recalls.

Chef Brooks made a conscious decision not to go to culinary school but to study in the real *labs* instead. His inaugural kitchen experience encouraged him to go abroad to work in France. He obtained jobs in Michelin star-rated kitchens where he reasoned, "I wanted to learn, so I would just ask for a place to stay and a wee bit o' money."

Ednam House is a casual hotel that particularly attracts wealthier fishermen, who can afford to spend literally thousands of dollars per week for the water rights to fish for salmon on the Tweed. It is not unusual to find the silvery body of a large, fresh-caught salmon on display in the hotel lobby. It is the talk of the day and the taste of the night at the table in the hotel dining room.

A view of the river can be had from every table in the eighty-seat dining room, which — in Ednam style — is casual and warm. The chef's menu changes nightly with three to four appetizers, a soup, three to four entrees, and sweets — including a daily choice of homemade ice cream. The food is full of flavor, and best described as rustic with a gourmet flair.

"I want to produce food that people want to eat," says the chef. "It doesn't matter how many stars a place has. It is not a chef's job to educate people, but to provide food that people can enjoy." To that end, he advises that home cooks should not be snobbish about their food. "Don't go overboard and buy expensive items. Buy them fresh and buy what you like."

Most of the salmon at Ednam House come from the Tweed, which stretches for ninety-four miles. Each year salmon battle their way upstream to reach spawning grounds they left some three years earlier. In the kitchen, only a few feet off the river banks, Ralph Brooks paddles his own upward course, working seven days a week with his hand in every pot to make sure that there is always a song at every table. ◆

Scotch Broth of Barley, Lamb, and Oatmeal

The Scottish people are passionate about soup. This one blends traditional ingredients such as lamb, barley, and oatmeal with fresh vegetables. It's perfect for a chilly evening supper.

1	tablespoon butter
2	medium onions, diced
2	medium carrots, diced or 1 cup
1	medium turnip, diced, or 1 cup
3	ribs celery, diced or 1 cup
2	cleaned leeks, diced
1/2	pound shoulder or neck of lamb meat, diced
2	quarts chicken stock or chicken broth
1	lamb shin bone
3/4	cup barley
1	tablespoon uncooked oatmeal (old-fashioned oats)
1/4	cup finely chopped parsley

In a 4-quart saucepan or stockpot, melt the butter. Add the onion, carrots, turnip, celery, leeks, and the lamb.

Cook over medium heat until the onion becomes tender and translucent and the lamb begins to turn brown.

Add the chicken stock and the shin bone. Then add the barley and the oatmeal, stirring as you go to prevent sticking. Bring the mixture to the boil and then turn down and simmer for 1 1/2 hours with the lid on the pot. (Note: You may soak the barley for five hours and bring the cooking time down to about 1/2 hour.) The soup is cooked when the barley is tender. Remove the shin bone, mix in the parsley and serve. Yield: 12 servings. ◆

Wine Suggestion

This sparkling wine is made by the traditional *méthode champenoise*. The toasty and creamy character of **Domaine Chandon Réserve** marries well with this soup and is an excellent accompaniment to smoked meats and fish, deep-fried foods, shellfish, and dishes featuring green or black olives.

Salmon Filets with Sorrel Sauce

Sorrel is actually in the herb family but it is often cooked as a vegetable. High in vitamin A and hefty amounts of vitamin C, calcium, and potassium, sorrel resembles spinach. In fact, if you cannot get fresh sorrel, substitute fresh spinach leaves for this recipe.

1	pound (4 filets) salmon
	Salt and pepper to taste
1/2	cup butter plus 1 tablespoon
8	ounces of sorrel or spinach, stalks removed
1	cup fish stock
1/2	cup cream
1	tablespoon lemon juice

Preheat the oven to 350°. Clean the salmon of its scales with the back of a knife. Clean the fish and score each filet from top to bottom to allow the flavor from the sauce to permeate the fish. Season the fish with salt and pepper. Melt 2 tablespoons of the butter in a skillet on high heat. Add the fish, skin-side down. Sear and turn over. Sear on the other side. Transfer the fish to a greased, 9x13-inch baking pan. Bake for 15 minutes or until the flesh is firm.

Meanwhile, prepare the sauce. Melt the remaining butter (except the 1 tablespoon) in a skillet over medium heat. Add the sorrel and stir constantly so that it does not stick. As soon as the leaves turn a gray-green (less than 2 minutes), remove from the pan. Place the sorrel and the fish stock into a blender. Whirl until fairly smooth.

 Pour the mixture into a medium saucepan. Add the cream and lemon juice. Salt to taste. Bring the mixture to a boil, stirring constantly, and then add the remaining tablespoon of butter. Pour the sauce over the fish and serve. Yield: 4 servings. ◆

Wine Suggestion

The richness and complex flavors of the Chardonnay grape, when married with the liveliness and fresh-fruit characteristics of Pinot Grigio, make **Libaio** a perfect companion to the salmon and sorrel dish.

> *I wanted to learn, so I would just ask for a place to stay and a wee bit o' money.*

CHEF RALPH BROOKS

Perched on the banks of Scotland's famous River Tweed, seared salmon is surrounded by a fresh sorrel sauce and accoutrements for a day of salmon fishing.

Butterscotch and Chocolate Tart

Scotland is known for its toffee-like desserts. This caramel special, carefully constructed by Chef Ralph Brooks, is only decadently enhanced by the chocolate. Serve with a scoop of vanilla ice cream.

═══════════════

Pastry:
2   cups all-purpose flour
$^1/_8$ teaspoon salt
1   cup sugar
1   cup butter
1   egg

Filling:
1   cup butter
1 $^1/_2$ cups golden syrup, butterscotch syrup, or caramel sauce
1   cup sugar
2   cups heavy cream
5   egg yolks

Topping:
1   cup quality dark chocolate
1   cup heavy cream

═══════════════

Preheat the oven to 350°. Prepare the pastry. In a mixing bowl, mix together the flour, salt, sugar, and butter. Mix with your fingers until the butter is totally incorporated. Make a well in the center of the bowl and add the egg. Fold the egg in with a rubber spatula. Using your hands, knead the mixture until a soft dough forms. Reserve excess dough for another recipe.

Sprinkle pastry board and rolling pin with flour. Roll out the dough to about $^1/_8$-inch thickness. Place it over a 9 $^1/_2$ x 1$^1/_2$-inch tart pan. Line the pan with the dough, using fingers coated with flour. Press the dough against the sides and bottom of the pan. Remove excess dough from the rim of the pan. Prick the bottom and sides of dough with a fork. Bake in the oven for about 15 to 20 minutes or until the crust is lightly browned and the pastry is firm. Remove from the oven and set aside.

Make the filling. In a medium saucepan, bring the butter, golden syrup, and sugar to a boil. Stir occasionally. When the mixture is smooth, about 4 minutes, stir in the cream and remove from the heat.

In a mixing bowl, whisk the egg yolks well. Add in half the syrup mixture, stirring as you pour. Then, pour the contents of the bowl into the saucepan containing the other half of the syrup. Cook under gentle heat, bringing the mixture just to the boil, stirring constantly to prevent sticking and keep the eggs from scrambling. As soon as the mixture boils, pour it into the tart crust. Bake in the oven for 25 to 30 minutes or until the pie is set and the center is not like jelly. The surface will be a little bubbly. Remove from the oven and set aside.

To prepare the topping, melt the chocolate over the stove in a double boiler. In a small saucepan, bring the cream to a boil. When the chocolate has melted, pour it into the cream and stir to combine. Remove from the heat. Pour the chocolate over the top of the tart. Place in the refrigerator to chill for at least 2 hours. Serve cold or at room temperature. Yield: 10 to 12 servings. ◆

Spirit Suggestion

The rarest of the Hennessy blends, **Paradis** (Paradise) is a sublime blend of very rich, older cognacs, some of which are more than one-hundred years old. Slow aging in old oak barrels accounts for the delicate aroma, rich complex flavors, and golden amber color. Silken in texture, Paradis is a treasure to be savored slowly with this rich, Scottish classic dessert.

Just down the street from Ednam House, the ruins of Kelso Abbey stand majestically along with an equally regal Butterscotch and Chocolate Tart from the chef's special recipe.

The Kelso Bagpipe Band can be found performing in front of the old town hall on many a summer evening.

Here's one reason Kelso is a frequent winner of Britain in Bloom awards.

Ruins, Rhododendrons, and a Taste of Scotland

Chef Ian MacDonald

BALBIRNIE HOUSE, FIFE

The reins of chefdom did not come easily. He had been working at it since childhood without realizing it. He fed the chickens. He gathered the eggs and milked the cows — before he went to school — and then milked the cows again after school. But that was the regimen that paved the way for what Ian MacDonald does so well today.

As executive chef of Balbirnie House, no one thinks what Ian does is just for girls, as in the days when cooking was first a gleam in his eye. Ian was shut out of cooking classes for girls until one year when they finally, grudgingly let him attend.

Today, he wins awards for his cooking, such as those from the worldwide culinary Olympics. In 1994, he and sixteen other Scottish chefs represented the United Kingdom and came home with ten gold medals, ten silver, and three bronze. Then he and his team clinched the best overall award in the world for a culinary team.

It is these talents that he brings to the unassuming yet elegant Balbirnie House, a 1777 Georgian country mansion that is the centerpiece of the 416-acre Balbirnie Park. The house's many changes throughout its sterling history are depicted on the odd-matched antique tables in the intimate Balbirnie dining room. Base hotplates at individual place settings showcase old photographs and etchings from postcards the current owners — the Russells — found and turned into the base mats.

They are just part of the charm of this gracious manor surrounded by one of Scotland's most important collections of rhododendrons, beautiful wildflower arbors, and prehistoric stone circles. "I knew as soon as I walked in the door that this was the place for me," recalls Chef MacDonald. "The architecture, the gardens, the furniture — I knew my food would reflect this house."

The chef's dishes mirror a sensitivity to today's free style and the emphasis on fresh and flavorful. Unleashing the secret of his culinary savvy, it is all in his philosophy: "Get to know your green grocer, your fishmonger, your butcher. Then, they will tell you what is fresh and a good buy. Also, try a new dish on your family first before serving it to dinner guests. You naturally get better the second time around."

Breakfast, too, is important at Balbirnie. "It is the last thing guests will remember as they leave here. It must be up to standards," insists Chef MacDonald, that old childhood discipline kicking in once again to make Balbirnie House shine. ◆

Avocados and Mushrooms with Béchamel and Gruyère Cheese

The nutty flavor of the avocado with the cheese and herbs, offers a delicious appetizer or a main course for lunch with a salad. The deep green-colored fruit contains only 138 calories per eight ounces. It contains plenty of vitamin C, thiamin, and riboflavin.

2   tablespoons butter
1   small onion, finely chopped
4   slices lean Canadian-style bacon, cut into $^1/_2$-inch dice
1   clove garlic, crushed
$^1/_2$ pound button mushrooms, cut into quarters
$^3/_4$ cup béchamel or white sauce (see page 211)
$^3/_4$ cup heavy cream

Salt and pepper
2   avocados (not too ripe)
1   egg yolk
2   tablespoons whipped cream
2   ounces Gruyère cheese, grated
4   sprigs fresh basil
4   sprigs marjoram, chopped

In a medium sauté pan, melt the butter and add the onions, bacon, and garlic. Cook for 1 minute over medium-high heat, or just until the vegetables begin to sweat. Add the mushrooms and cook, stirring occasionally, for 1 minute. Add the béchamel sauce and the heavy cream. Season with salt and pepper to taste. Simmer the mixture over medium heat for 5 minutes.

Meanwhile, peel the avocados, remove the stones, and chop the fruit into $^1/_2$-inch pieces. Add the avocado to the sauté pan and simmer for 2 more minutes. Remove from the heat.

In a small bowl, gently beat the egg yolk into the whipped cream. Fold this liaison mixture or thickening agent into the avocado mixture. Pour the mixture into individual serving bowls and sprinkle with Gruyère cheese. Pass under the grill or broiler for a few seconds to allow the cheese to brown lightly. Garnish with a sprig of basil and marjoram. Yield: 4 servings. ◆

Wine Suggestion

A dish such as the Avocado and Mushrooms with Béchamel and Gruyère Cheese contains a wide variety of flavors and textures that come together when served with the luscious and aromatic Fitz-Ritter dry **Gewürztraminer.**

The Balbirnie House avocado-and-mushroom dish

Smoked Chicken Ravioli with Red Pepper Sauce

These ravioli are full of flavor and texture, and the red pepper sauce is a gentle accompaniment to the smoked chicken. You may get smoked chicken from your butcher or at specialty stores. Sometimes small local restaurants that smoke meats will do the same for you. You may also substitute with unsmoked meat that you have seasoned with your choice of herbs and spices, or try smoked turkey.

Ravioli Dough:
- 1 pound all-purpose flour
- 4 eggs
- 2 teaspoons warm water
- 2 teaspoons olive oil
- 1 teaspoon salt
- $\frac{1}{8}$ teaspoon nutmeg
- 1 egg white for wash

Filling:
- 8 ounces smoked chicken
- $\frac{1}{4}$ cup heavy cream
- $\frac{1}{2}$ red bell pepper, roasted
- Salt and pepper

Sauce:
- 1 $\frac{1}{2}$ large red bell peppers, roasted and skinned
- $\frac{1}{4}$ cup unsalted butter
- 1 shallot, chopped
- $\frac{1}{4}$ cup Riesling wine
- $\frac{1}{4}$ cup chicken stock
- $\frac{3}{4}$ cup (scant) heavy cream
- Salt and pepper

Garnish:
- $\frac{1}{4}$ cup freshly chopped chives

Begin by making the ravioli dough. Place all of the ravioli-dough ingredients into a food processor and mix thoroughly until a dough forms. Place ball of dough into a bowl, cover with a tea towel and let rest for 3 hours or in the refrigerator if resting overnight.

Next day, make the filling. Finely dice enough chicken to yield $\frac{1}{4}$ cup. Set aside. Blend the remainder of the chicken in a processor along with $\frac{1}{4}$ cup of the heavy cream. Process coarsely to make the filling. Finely chop the $\frac{1}{2}$ of the bell pepper. Add it to the filling, mixing it in well. Add the diced chicken. Season the mixture with salt and pepper to taste. Place the mixture in the refrigerator. Remove dough from the refrigerator if resting overnight. Let rest on a counter for $\frac{1}{2}$ hour before kneading.

Knead the ravioli dough, stretching it to about $\frac{1}{8}$-inch thickness or thinner, using a pasta machine. Cut dough into 3-inch circles using a round biscuit cutter. Place 1 scant tablespoon of the mixture into

continued on page 117

Vaulted ceilings rise to the occasion in the gallery at Balbirnie House where the chef has dished up a scrumptious Smoked Chicken Ravioli with Red Pepper Sauce.

the center of each circle. Brush the dough outside of the filling with egg white. Fold the pastry over tightly, forming the circle into a half-moon shape. Repeat until all of the mixture is used up. Place on a flat tray in the refrigerator just until you make the sauce.

Make the sauce by first placing the red peppers into a blender. Whirl for about 1 minute or until puréed. Place 1 tablespoon of the butter in a medium saucepan over medium heat. Add the shallot and cook gently. Add the wine once the shallot has turned translucent. Raise the heat and allow the wine to reduce by $1/2$. Follow with the chicken stock and reduce by $1/2$ again. Add the heavy cream and the red pepper purée. Add the remaining butter and salt and pepper to taste. Allow the mixture to cook until the butter melts. Stir well. Keep warm.

Bring a large saucepan of water to the boil. Remove the ravioli from the refrigerator and cook them in the water for 3 to 4 minutes or until al dente. Drain.

Place some of the sauce on an individual serving plate and add 5 ravioli per plate. Cover with more sauce and garnish with chopped chives. Yield: 20 ravioli or 4 appetizer servings. ◆

Wine Suggestion

The light, black-cherry aroma from Pinot Meunier grapes, a fresh raspberry-like character from the classic Pinot Noir, and a spicy opulence and smooth texture imparted by the Cabernet Franc, make **Simi Altaire** a delicious and flavorful choice for this well-seasoned dish.

Brilliant fields of a flower known as rape *– grown for its cooking oil – bring the Fife countryside alive with color. The flowers are almost identical to the mustard flowers that grow all over Europe.*

Victorian Resort Works Out with Spa Cuisine

Chef Stewart Cameron

TURNBERRY HOTEL, AYRSHIRE

Turbulent dunes and rocky crags are tamed by the sprawling splendor of the famous Turnberry resort, along Scotland's southwest coast. Holidays by the sea in a stately, whitewashed and tawny-roofed hotel suggest a quieter time when ladies wore straw hats and oxford shoes and men wore knickers and riding caps to swing a club over at Turnberry's famous links.

Golfers from all over the world watch in wonder during the British Open, played here against the contrasting azure waters on one side and verdant pasturelands on the other.

Turnberry, on its 360 acres, is in a world of

its own, quite set apart from busy towns or even small villages.

When you come here, you come to stay and be one with the sea. The hotel's environs invite the adventurous as well as the meditative. The hotel is also known for its spa where guests can spend a day in therapy and massage rooms; swim in a heated, glassed-in pool; experience mud wraps and hydrobaths; and end the day either in the hotel's luxurious, gilded and chandelier-studded dining room or at the more informal Bay at Turnberry Restaurant.

Chef Stewart Cameron is the executive chef at Turnberry, and I asked him to give *World Class Cuisine* a sample of the food served at the Bay Restaurant where the spa is also housed. It is the hotel's lighter fare, featuring many items prepared on the grill right in the dining room itself.

Although less formal than the other dining room, the restaurant by the bay is still casually elegant with breathtaking views of rugged windswept coastline along the golf course. Chef Cameron offers the Mussel and Scampi Risotto as one of the dishes that he says satisfies diners who want something light. In fact, there are several risotto choices on the menu, and they may be ordered as appetizers or as main courses.

Chef Cameron grew up on a farm in the Perthshire region of Scotland. "Growing up on a farm — surrounded by the freshest ingredients — you get an appreciation for what good food really should be," says the chef. That makes for a perfect match for the Bay Restaurant, even though the chef is in charge of all three dining areas — including another one at the Turnberry clubhouse.

The chef knew from his farming days that he always wanted to work with food. So he served an apprenticeship in the early Sixties, working in the Caledonian in Edinburgh. From there, he oversaw kitchens in many prestigious hotels in Scotland and earned a reputation, not only for his cuisine, but also for being one of the industry's great culinary teachers. ◆

Mussel and Scampi Risotto

The rich creaminess of the risotto combines with the shellfish to make a delicious entree. Use the smaller mussels as they tend to be much more tender than the large. When cleaning the mussels, be sure to scrub the shells under cold water. When purchasing mussels, be sure the shells are closed and discard any that open before preparation. Risotto is a rewarding rice to cook. The slow method of cooking it — adding liquid and waiting for it to evaporate — yields a creamy rice, making it a meal in itself when vegetables or pieces of meat are added.

===

Preparation:
40   small mussels, cleaned and bearded
1   cup white wine
    Juice of ½ lemon
2   tablespoons chopped shallots

Risotto:
4   cups fish stock
8   medium shrimp, cleaned and deveined
2   tablespoons sunflower oil
2   shallots, peeled and finely diced
1   pound Arborio rice
½   cup unsalted butter
½   cup grated Parmesan cheese
2   tablespoons chopped fresh oregano or 1 tablespoon dried
    Salt and pepper
    Bunch of dill for garnish

===

First, prepare the mussels. In a large stockpot, add the wine, lemon juice, and shallots. Add the mussels and the lid of the pan and steam the shellfish for about 5 minutes or just until they open. Remove them from the shell. Strain the liquid and set aside. You may use this if you need to add more liquid to the cooking rice.

continued on page 120

Heat the fish stock and poach the shrimp for about 1 minute. Remove from stock with a slotted spoon. Remove stock from heat, cool down, and reserve.

In a 4-quart saucepan, heat the oil and sweat the shallots for about 1 minute, or just until they are translucent. Add the rice and cook another 2 minutes, stirring constantly to prevent sticking.

Add 1 cup of the fish stock. Bring it to a boil and then simmer, stirring frequently, until the liquid is absorbed. Continue adding the stock the same way at intervals until the rice has almost cooked, about 25 minutes. While the rice is still al dente, blend in the butter, Parmesan cheese, oregano, and mussels. Season with salt and pepper.

Portion the rice and mussels onto serving plates. Decorate with the shrimp and the dill. Yield: 4 servings. ◆

Wine Suggestion

Cabreo La Pietra Chardonnay, from the *Tuscan Estates of Ruffino,* is a mouth-filling wine, with a richness of fruit that perfectly accents the Mussel and Scampi Risotto.

The Turnberry pool and spa is the setting for this delicious Mussel and Scampi Risotto.

Beef with Shiitake Mushrooms and Madeira Sauce with Garlic-Scented Potatoes

The meat and potatoes are all in one, so this is a great dish for a dinner party. The truffle oil in this recipe really gives the beef an intense flavor but olive oil is a fine substitute. You may make the Madeira sauce ahead of time.

Madeira Sauce:

- 2 tablespoons sunflower oil
- ½ cup vegetable mirepoix or mixture of chopped onion, carrot, and celery
- 2 tablespoons mixture of chopped basil and oregano or other mixture of desired herbs
- 1 cup chopped beef (filet mignon preferred) trimmings
- 2 cups Madeira
- 1 tablespoon tomato paste
- 4 cups quality beef stock

Potatoes:

- 2 large potatoes, peeled and cut julienne
- 2 cloves garlic, crushed
- 2 tablespoons chopped herbs (parsley, thyme, chives) Salt and pepper
- 2 tablespoons sunflower oil

Beef:

- ½ cup truffle oil or olive oil
- 4 7-ounce pieces beef (filet mignon preferred), cut in half
- 8 ounces shiitake mushrooms
- 1 cup peeled, blanched, and diced shallots

Prepare the sauce first. In a large skillet, heat the oil and add the mirepoix, herbs, and the beef trimming. Add the Madeira. Cook over medium-high heat until the liquid evaporates, about 25 minutes. Add the tomato paste. Stir in the beef stock and bring to the boil. Stir and skim off beef and mirepoix. Reduce until you have half the quantity of the sauce, about 20 minutes. Strain through a cheesecloth or fine-mesh strainer. Keep warm.

Preheat the oven to 350°. The style of preparing the potatoes is rosti where thin strips of potato cook in oil and the starch helps them stick together, forming a patty or a base upon which to place the meat. Mix the strips of raw potato with garlic, herbs, and the salt and pepper to taste, and form into 4 patties. In an ovenproof medium skillet, heat the oil in a nonstick pan and cook the potatoes, until crisp. Turn over when browned and cook on the other side. Set aside. Put the skillet into the oven and cook for 5 minutes.

Prepare the beef next. Brush a grilling pan with some of the truffle oil or olive oil. Grill the meat to desired doneness. Meanwhile, heat the remaining oil in a medium skillet and sauté the shiitake mushrooms with the shallots. Season lightly with salt and pepper. Cook until the mushrooms are al dente.

To assemble, place the hot potatoes onto individual serving plates. Place two pieces of the beef per plate, just off the side of the potatoes. Drape the Madeira sauce all around the plate. Serve immediately. Yield: 4 servings. ◆

Wine Suggestion

A skillful blend of the classic Bordeaux varietals, **Simi Cabernet Sauvignon Reserve** exhibits rich and complex aromas and flavors of cherry, cedar, and black currant. Extended aging in French oak barrels helps to create a smooth and very elegant wine that underscores the hearty flavors of the beef and the shiitake mushrooms.

A beef and mushroom entree is a golfer's delight at the Turnberry resort, frequent home of the prestigious British Open.

Cooking in the 'Engine Room' of a Baronial Mansion

Chef David Hunt

AUCHTERARDER HOUSE, AUCHTERARDER

His memories of childhood are not of kicking a white-and-black ball between the goalposts or packing up his books and going off to school. When David Hunt was growing up, he could wrangle with the toughest of his chums in the neighborhood and compete at many sports with much success. But what stands out the most in his early years is the impression food had on him.

"Sundays were baking days and my mother made a huge breakfast. The rest of the day, a big pot o' broth would boil away with spices and seasonings, ham knuckles, barley, leeks, and carrots, and it would stew away for hours," he recalls.

One day, the chef's mother found him at the kitchen counters, flour everywhere and ingredients from cupboards and refrigerator all in a bowl, as he attempted to make dinner with a recipe in his head. "The place was a shambles," he remembers. "I think cooking was always in my blood." He went on to study at Glasgow and Perth catering colleges and then went to work at several country house hotels before coming to Auchterarder.

Today, his wife does the cooking at home. But at Auchterarder House, "a place we call a home and not a hotel," as their slogan says, David is the head chef in the kitchen he calls the engine room.

It's very hot back there, but the engine room nickname stems more from the chef's outlook. He believes the kitchen is the heart of the home at Auchterarder. To that end, he works as a team with a *commis* chef, a *chef de partie,* and several other cooks who work as a well-oiled machine, with everyone's wheels spinning and turning in harmony.

As the engine room pumps away, Auchterarder guests are in for a special treat. Rather than sitting right down to dinner, they have the option to relax in one of the home's many splendid common rooms, including a paneled library, stone and glass conservatory, or cocktail lounge. This is where they have a drink and are presented with the menu, ordering from wherever they sit, rather than at the table. Then when the food is just about ready, they are escorted to the intimate, twenty-six-seat dining room.

Regional oil and watercolor paintings are the highlight of the room, which was the original dining room for the house, circa 1832, when a lieutenant colonel and his family built the home. Today guests of the highly praised historic home enjoy David Hunt's food. His fare is French-influenced Scottish cuisine that may include Angus Beef Crowned with Horseradish and Herb Crumble with a Rosemary and Port Sauce or a Smoked Salmon with Yogurt Quenelles in a Garlic and Coriander Sauce — indeed, a long way from a "big pot o' broth." ◆

Warm Salad of Scallops and Langoustines with Snow Peas and Raspberry Vinegar

Scotland is famous for its shellfish. The sweetness of the fish here is matched by the sharpness of the raspberry vinegar.

1/4 cup raspberry vinegar
3/4 cup walnut oil
2 tablespoons vegetable oil
8 sea scallops, cleaned and cut in half

1 pound langoustines or shrimp, cleaned
1/2 cup carrot, cut julienne style, blanched
1/2 cup snow peas, blanched
   Salt and pepper
   Assortment of about 1/2 pound lettuce: endive, radicchio, iceberg

Prepare the raspberry dressing by whisking the vinegar with the walnut oil in a medium bowl. Set aside.

Heat a skillet with the vegetable oil and add the scallops and scampi. Cook very quickly for 1 minute, turning the shellfish to cook on all sides. Stir in the carrots and snow peas. Remove from the pan but reserve the pan, setting aside the shellfish and vegetables in a bowl in a warm place.

Divide the lettuce among 4 individual serving plates. Season with salt and pepper.

Return the skillet to the stove and deglaze the pan with the raspberry dressing. Heat through.

Arrange the shellfish and vegetable mixture on top of the lettuce and then coat with the warm dressing. Serve immediately. Yield: 4 servings. ◆

Scallops and langoustines are the stars of this seafood favorite at Auchterarder House. The dish is flavored with a raspberry sauce laced with walnuts and served here on a Scottish tartan in the conservatory.

Hot Apple Tart with Apricot Jam and Caramel Sauce

The chef considers this apple dish an "up-market" apple pie. It certainly makes for an elegant dessert, and it's easy to do. The caramel cage is optional but makes for a lovely garnish. You may also make this dish as larger tarts, using a 6-inch round cutter and cutting the tarts up to serve, as in photo.

Tart:
- 3 McIntosh apples, peeled, cored, and cut in half
- 6 3-inch, round, thin disks of puff pastry
- 3 teaspoons sugar
- 1/4 cup butter

Glaze:
- 2 tablespoons apricot jam
- 2 tablespoons water

Sauce:
- 1/2 cup plus 1 tablespoon sugar
- 1/4 cup water
- 1/2 cup heavy cream

Caramel Cage Garnish:
- 1 tablespoon corn syrup
- 1 cup sugar

Preheat the oven to 400°. Partially bake pastry for 15 minutes. Cut the apples into very thin slices. Arrange overlapping over the pastry disks. Add the sugar and dot with butter. Set aside. Reduce oven to 325°.

In a small saucepan, boil together the apricot jam and the water until it forms a glaze-like texture. Pass through a sieve. Spread overtop the apples and pastry. Bake for 12 to 15 minutes more or until the pastry is a light golden brown. Place under a broiler or grill for 1 minute, just to caramelize.

While the tarts bake in the oven, prepare the caramel sauce. In a medium saucepan, combine the sugar with the water and bring to a boil, cooking gently until the mixture thickens and resembles a light toffee. In a small saucepan, bring the heavy cream to a boil and then add it to the thickened caramel, stirring well.

To make the caramel cage, heat the corn syrup and sugar together. Drizzle the syrup over the bottom of the bowl of a ladle. Allow to harden and cool. Remove carefully from the ladle.

When serving the apple tarts, surround the serving plate with the sauce. Top with vanilla ice cream if desired and crown with the caramel cage. Yield: 6 servings. ◆

Wine Suggestion

The savory bouquet of cinnamon, raisins, and figs found in the **Moët & Chandon Demi-Sec** champagne is especially well suited to Chef Hunt's fruit-filled tart. The richness and soft style even complement the lush caramel sauce.

A filigree cage of caramelized sugar tops this delicious tart filled with apples and apricot jam, floating in a buttery caramel sauce on the grounds of this elegant Victorian mansion. (This version is made with 6-inch pastry rounds.)

Old Country Mill Now Churns Out Passion and Award-Winning Cooking

Chef Nick Nairn

BRAEVAL OLD MILL RESTAURANT, ABERFOYLE

Cooking was never a glint in Nick Nairn's bright eyes. It was not until he bought a house that he realized he had to use the kitchen, and so he bought a cookbook. "I taught myself how to boil an egg," he shares, of his first culinary venture. Today, he holds one of a restaurant's highest honors — the Michelin star, earned only a few years after that first egg bubbled successfully on his stovetop.

To summarize how it all happened and so quickly, one would have to say that Nick Nairn used his heart and soul as his guide. Cooking caught hold of him and he found that he wanted to share his passion. "At twenty-three, there I was on a Saturday, poring through cookbooks, planning an evening meal for friends," says Nick. "Can you imagine that?"

Two years later, he found a wreck of an eighteenth-century threshing mill and hatched the idea of opening a restaurant. His supportive girlfriend Fiona, who later became his wife, encouraged the move, and Nick took a year to work on it with his own hands: rebuilding walls, replacing the slate roof, adding the electricity, and installing a water system.

Now, eight years later, diners come from miles away to this farmer's territory to eat at Nick Nairn's table. "It's a funny location for what we do," describes the chef. The thirty-two-

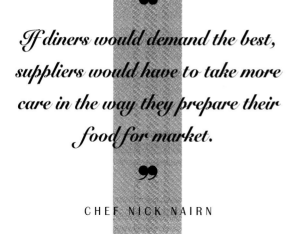

passions to the table in his own way, is really rather rare in the world. So it is no wonder why guests trek their way to the old mill to see what Nick Nairn is churning up on any given day. ◆

Carrot Soup with Honey and Ginger

The ginger and honey in this otherwise traditional carrot soup literally make all of the difference in the world. Chef Nairn's touch for the Oriental is very evident. The soup is easy to make and can be frozen ahead of time. Just eliminate the garnish until ready to serve.

seat room has a daily menu, because Nick never knows what he is going to cook until he finds the food. The chef insists on only the best meats and produce. If salmon, for example, does not have "bulging eyes, pink gills and firm flesh," then, to put it in his words, "they aren't the boys for me."

Nick adds: "If diners would demand the best, suppliers would have to take more care in the way they prepare their food for market."

He sometimes credits his passions to his country roots. Having grown up only four miles from the mill, the chef's values are deep-rooted in integrity. He never took a cooking lesson, yet he continues to receive culinary awards. Perhaps it is because he is doing what he truly loves. "People have asked me to take over bigger, busier places, but I feel a sense of oneness here," says the chef, who makes the most of surrounding country trails as an avid cyclist.

Nick Nairn says most chefs cook from the recipes of others, but eventually inject their own personalities into their food. Thus, their own creations and cooking philosophies develop. He says that what he is doing — the adventuresome lack of a menu at a place in the middle of nowhere — "is rare in this country." But that, plus the opportunity to bring his loves and

10	cups water
1 ½	cups butter
3	medium onions, peeled and thinly sliced
2	tablespoons grated ginger root
12	turns of freshly ground pepper
3	teaspoons sea salt
3	pounds carrots, peeled and shredded
	Juice of ⅓ small lemon
¼	cup plus 1 tablespoon quality honey

Garnish:

½	cup heavy cream
¼	cup fresh chives

Place a large Dutch oven on the stove with 10 cups of water. Bring the water to a boil and keep it warm on the stovetop.

In a separate stockpot, add the butter and onions and cook over medium-high heat until the onions turn translucent. Add the ginger to the pot. Season with salt and pepper to taste. Add the shredded carrots to the stockpot and mix well to combine the ingredients. Squeeze in the juice from the lemon and pour in the honey. Stir the mixture well to blend.

Pour in the 10 cups of hot water and cook the

continued on page 131

The curiously carved pitchfork contrasts the inner stone walls of the restaurant. Carrot Soup with Honey and Ginger (on the curved-back chair) is one of Nick Nairn's specialties de la maison.

The vintage steamer SS Sir Walter Scott has been plying the waters of nearby Loch Katrine for nearly 100 years.

soup on a gentle, rolling boil for 45 minutes. When the soup is cooked and the carrots are tender, transfer the soup into a food processor in batches and purée until smooth. Dish the soup out into individual serving bowls and add a little cream to each bowl, running it through with a butter knife or spatula. Garnish with the chives. Yield: 10 servings. ◆

An old threshing mill in the middle of the Scottish countryside is the location of choice for renowned Chef Nick Nairn and his intimate bistro-style restaurant. Nage marinates in a jar while the salmon ingredients await the skillet.

Escalopes of Salmon with an Avocado-and-Tomato Compote in a Basil Sauce

Chef Nairn uses his own version of a nage, which is made here with vegetables and a variety of spices. Nage in a recipe usually indicates a court-bouillon that will be used in a seafood dish. In this case, it is comprised of diced vegetables that will marinate in the liquid, be drained, and form the basis for a sauce. Prepare the nage two days in advance.

Nage:

1	medium onion, diced
1	leek, white part only, diced
1	rib celery, diced
4	large carrots, diced
1	head garlic, diced
$\frac{1}{3}$	teaspoon white pepper, crushed
1	star anise
1	bay leaf
2	tablespoons mixed herbs: coriander, chervil, parsley, tarragon, thyme
1	cup quality white wine

continued on page 132

Sauce:

- 2 cups plus 2 tablespoons nage
- ¼ cup unsalted butter, diced
- 1 teaspoon lemon juice
  Juice of ¼ small lemon
  Salt and pepper
- 18 fresh basil leaves, chopped and added at the last minute

Avocado Compote:

- 1 large ripe avocado
- 2 ripe plum tomatoes
  Juice of 1 lime
- 1 tablespoon extra virgin olive oil
- ⅛ teaspoon each worcestershire sauce and tabasco

Salmon:

- 2 tablespoons peanut oil
- 6 (3-ounce) filets salmon
  Juice of 1 lemon

Wine Suggestion

Named after the Benedictine monk Pierre Pérignon, who is credited with discovering the famous *champagne method,* **Cuvée Dom Pérignon** is a profound champagne with a taste of acacia honey and fruit. It is a regal accompaniment to any fine meal, especially with a dish that contains myriad flavors as does the escalope of salmon.

To prepare the nage, add the diced vegetables to a 2-quart stockpot with enough water (about 4 ½ cups) to cover the vegetables. Simmer over medium-high heat for about 8 minutes. Add the herbs and spices and simmer for another 2 minutes, then add the wine. Remove the pot from the heat and allow to cool. Place in a storage container and marinate for 48 hours, then strain off the liquid.

Meanwhile, prepare the sauce. In a medium saucepan, reduce the nage to about 1 ½ cups by cooking over medium-high heat. It will take about 20 minutes. Whisk in the butter. Add the lemon juice. Season with salt and pepper. Pass through a sieve. Keep warm.

Make the compote by peeling the avocado and dicing it. Blanch, skin, and quarter the tomatoes; remove the seeds, dice, and mix with the avocado. Add the oil, juice, worcestershire, and tabasco. Set aside.

In a large skillet, heat the peanut oil and sauté the fish for 2 minutes until crisp. Fish should have a seared appearance and be dark at the edges. Remove from the pan and place uncooked side down. Squeeze lemon juice overall and sprinkle with salt and pepper.

Place a dollop of the avocado compote in the center of the plate. Add the chopped basil to the sauce. Pour the sauce all around and then place the salmon on top. Yield: 4 to 6 servings. ◆

When he's not in the kitchen, Chef Nairn loves to ride his mountain bike over the hilly terrain that surrounds the restaurant.

Fare That Is More Than Par for the Course in Golf's Homeland

Chef Alan Hill

GLENEAGLES RESORT, PERTHSHIRE

"Judge who is coming to dinner and design your menu accordingly," is the advice Chef Alan Hill has for the home cook. That is his main job at Gleneagles. For food is served here in the elegant, neoclassical Strathearn Dining Room, the cozy Dormy House at the country club, and the informal Equestrian Center.

Chef Hill approaches his work as though he is cooking for his very own guests. That is the philosophy he has instilled in the kitchens at Gleneagles, where some seventy chefs take Alan Hill's cue.

"Home cooking is like commercial cooking in that we have the same problems and have to find the solutions that allow us to offer our best face and food to our guests," explains Hill, one of Scotland's most-renowned chefs.

Alan Hill suggests making the starter course the day before, as well as a light soup. "Then the day of the dinner party, once you have fed your guests the appetizer and soup, they won't miss you as you go into the kitchen and spend a little time on the main course."

The element of surprise is also nice for entertaining, suggests this easy-going chef, who relishes his life as an executive chef and host to thousands who come to golf or just relax at Gleneagles — one of the world's most famous golf resorts. "Think about doing what we do in The Strathearn. Roll in your tea table or place the roast on your sideboard and carve it in front of your guests," he suggests. "It's all about pampering and good taste."

Chef Hill is steadfast about using Scottish ingredients in his cooking and enjoys blending traditional recipes with modern styles. You will find him using Scotch in his cooking as some chefs use wine. (See page 139 for more on cooking with Scotch.) "Scotch tenderizes your food as well as adds a delicate flavor. It is extremely versatile," he notes. The Scottish Queen of Puddings, for example, incorporates whisky in this most delicate dessert.

The championship golf courses at Gleneagles (there are now three courses, including a new one designed by Jack Nicklaus) have been the swinging stage for royalty and celebrities, who have hailed the game since it was invented in the fifteenth century at nearby St. Andrews, Scotland. Chef Hill admits he seldom gets to golf as his time is taken up by cooking for those who want great fare as well as great fairways. His time on the skeet shooting range at Gleneagles is also understandably limited. While earning such awards as Scottish Master Chef of 1985 and high entries in all of the prestigious food/travel guides, he is more likely to be found with a pen and wire whisk in hand than a putter or a firearm.

Probably the best advice this chef has for the home cook is what comes so naturally to him: "Let your feelings and your love of food and cooking come out from your fingers right onto the plate." ◆

> " Think about doing what we do in The Strathearn. Roll in your tea table or place the roast on your sideboard and carve it in front of your guests. It's all about pampering and good taste. "
>
> CHEF ALAN HILL

Teeing off on the first hole of the King's Course at Gleneagles with a traditional Scottish dish of Musselberg Pie (The lattice top is puff pastry crusted with oatmeal.) Shown here with Ruffino's Libaio white wine, this beef-and-seafood dish is especially well matched with the red Ruffino Torgaio Sangiovese. (See wine suggestion on page 136.)

Steak, Oyster, and Mussel Pie with Red Wine Sauce and Oatmeal Pastry

In Scotland, they call this traditional dish Musselberg Pie. Here, Chef Alan Hill offers a gourmet rendition that makes a lovely presentation. Served with a fresh vegetable salad, this hearty, stew-like casserole makes a well-rounded dinner. Choose mussels that are not opened. Scrub mussels and remove beards under cold water.

4	ounces large mussels, cleaned and bearded
1	cup white wine
	Salt and pepper
1/4	cup vegetable oil
2	tablespoons mixture of chopped rosemary and thyme
2	tablespoons butter
1/4	cup chopped onion
1	garlic clove, finely chopped
1/4	cup red wine
1	cup beef stock (may be purchased fresh/frozen)
1	cup brown sauce (see page 212 or make from a packaged mix)
1 1/2	pounds tender cut beef filets (filet mignon preferred)
16	oysters
1	tablespoon chopped parsley

Pastry:

2	sheets prepared puff pastry
1	egg, beaten for egg wash
1/4	cup ground, toasted oatmeal (old-fashioned oats)

Steam the mussels in the white wine and lemon juice in a large stockpot until they open (about 5 minutes). Remove the shells and discard. Set the mussels aside.

Trim and cut the steak into 1-inch cubes. Season the meat with salt and pepper. In a large skillet, heat the oil over medium-high heat. Brown the meat on all sides, adding the herbs during the cooking process. Remove from the heat after the meat is seared and set aside.

In another skillet, melt the butter and cook the onions and garlic until lightly browned. Deglaze the pan with the red wine. Add the beef stock and reduce the liquid by half. Add the brown sauce and the steak and cook the meat until tender (about 2 minutes).

Shell the oysters, saving their juice. Using a 1 1/2 to 2-quart oval casserole, pour in the cooked meat with the juices. Fold in the mussels and arrange the oysters on top. Pour in the oyster juice and the chopped parsley.

Preheat the oven to 350°. Prepare the pastry topping. Roll out a puff pastry sheet to 1/4-inch thickness. Brush with egg wash. Brush the rim of the casserole dish with the egg wash. Place the pastry overtop the dish and trim the excess dough. Using a lattice pastry cutter, cut out the lattice top from the other piece of pastry. Place it over the crust and sprinkle the entire top with the toasted oatmeal. Bake 30 to 40 minutes or until the crust is golden brown. Yield: 4 servings. ◆

Wine Suggestion

The often perplexing search for a wine that can work well with both steak and shellfish is over. The Sangiovese grape lends a delicate perfume to this light and fresh wine that is rich in fruit character. **Ruffino Torgaio Sangiovese** has just the right texture and refreshing taste to combine well with the steak, oysters, and mussels found in Chef Alan Hill's traditional Scottish pie.

The Gleneagles dining room looks out on the garden, where any time is right for the Scottish Queen of Puddings dessert.

Scottish Queen of Puddings

The look of this sweet resembles the soft, furry white and gem-studded cape of a queen on her throne. It tastes superb and is fun to make. It combines a spongecake with a custard and jam, a touch of whisky, and a meringue top. Most of Scotland's puddings were peasant recipes created from scraps. Later, however, puddings became the fare of royalty such as this one favored by Mary Queen of Scots.

Sauce:

- $3/4$ cup milk
- $1/2$ teaspoon vanilla extract
- $1/3$ cup plus 1 tablespoon sugar
- $1/2$ cup heavy cream
- $1/8$ teaspoon nutmeg
- 5 egg yolks
- 1 tablespoon quality single-malt whisky, such as Dalwhinnie

continued on page 138

Cake:

- 1   8-inch, single-layer vanilla sponge-type cake, such as angel's food, cut into 1-inch chunks (purchase or see page 212)
- ¼   cup plus 1 tablespoon quality single-malt whisky such as Dalwhinnie
- ¼   cup sultanas or raisins
- ¾   cup cherry glacé or cherry filling

Custard:

- 1   cup heavy cream
- ½   cup sugar
- 4   eggs, slightly beaten

Glaze:

- ¼   cup raspberry jam
- 1   tablespoon quality single-malt whisky such as Dalwhinnie

Meringue:

- 5   egg whites
- ¼   teaspoon salt
- ½   cup sugar

Garnish:

Maraschino cherries for garnish, if desired

Begin the dessert by preparing the cream sauce that accompanies the pudding. In a medium saucepan over medium heat, add the milk, vanilla, and sugar. Stir well. Heat just until the sugar dissolves. (You will use the remainder of the sauce ingredients later.)

Meanwhile, preheat the oven to 325°. Place the cake into a 6-cup, oval baking dish. Pour the ¼ cup plus 1 tablespoon of whisky evenly over the cake. Add the raisins and the cherry glacé. Set aside.

Make the custard. Pour the 1 cup heavy cream into a small saucepan and whisk in the sugar and then the eggs. Heat just until the sugar dissolves and the mixture is smooth, less than 2 minutes. Pour the custard over the cake in the oval dish. Bake the pudding in a bain marie in the oven for about 30 to 40 minutes or until the pudding is set and lightly browned.

While the pudding bakes, return to the sauce in progress on the stove. Add the cream, nutmeg, and whisk in the egg yolks aggressively. Add the whisky. Continue to cook on the stove over low to medium heat until the sauce thickens, about 20 minutes. Stir occasionally.

In a small saucepan, over low heat, cook the jam with 1 tablespoon of whisky. Remove the cake from the oven and ladle jam glaze overtop, spreading across the pudding evenly.

In a medium bowl with mixer at high speed, beat the egg whites and the salt for the meringue until stiff peaks form. Sprinkle the sugar into the meringue 2 tablespoons at a time, while mix begins to thicken, beating after each addition until sugar dissolves. Scoop the meringue into a pastry bag fitted with a decorative tip. Pipe the meringue around the entire edge of the pudding and then criss-cross back and forth in the middle of the pudding (see photo on page 137). Place the dish under a broiler for about 20 to 30 seconds, just to brown the tips of the meringue. Top with cherries, if desired.

Serve the pudding with the cream sauce immediately. Yield: 6 to 8 servings. ◆

Spirit Suggestion

While a single-malt Scotch whisky might not accompany the dessert, it remains an essential ingredient of this and many other Scottish recipes. The gently fragrant, 15-year-old **Dalwhinnie** single malt would most certainly be used in the celebration of milestones, and may offer your dinner guests a surprise touch.

Cooking with the Water of Life
Scotch Whisky in the Kitchen

A splash of white wine. A sprinkling of red Bordeaux. A dash of Madeira. Wines have always been the choice as alcoholic flavor enhancers to a variety of recipes. But the Scots employ the grain as much as the grape. In Scotland, Scotch whisky is enjoyed as a social libation, but it is perhaps in cooking where it is used most universally.

Splashes, sprinkles, and dashes of Scotch whisky provide the chef and the home cook with an added essence for everything from soups and vegetables to meat dishes and sweet desserts. Single malts are actually paired with recipes based on how peaty, heathery or delicate they are. No one knows that better than *World Class Cuisine's* Chef Alan Hill from Gleneagles in Perthshire.

"Scotch tenderizes food and also adds superb flavor. The taste is distinctive in the final dish," says the chef, who has been lauded by food writers for his exceptional use of the ubiquitous spirit. He patronizes the beverage for the way it "comforts a dish, shrouds it in warmth and caring." We can see that here in Alan Hill's Dalwhinnie Custard and his Marinated Salmon with Dill and Horseradish Salsa. (See also the chef's Scottish Queen of Puddings on page 137.)

Scotch whisky celebrated its five-hundredth anniversary in 1994, but no one knows for sure when the first drop was distilled as it was made without approval for centuries. The earliest record shows in 1494 that a delivery from King James IV of "eight bolls (one ton) of malt to make aquavitae" went to Cistercian Friar John Cor at an abbey in Fife. *Aquavitae* means *water of life* in Latin and is derived from the Gaelic *uisge beatha,* the wording which eventually evolved into *whisky* as the Scots spell it. And so it is, that a holy monk created the first official registration of a Scotch whisky producer.

Today, it is said that Scotland remains the only country able to produce the true Scotch whisky due to its unique, lush, green barley fields, crystal clear springs and ancient heather-scented peat bogs. This conducive environment imparts the unique flavors required to successfully make the spirit.

Single-malt Scotch whisky is touted as the top-of-the-line Scotch. Blended whiskys may contain as many as thirty to fifty different Scotches. Single malts are made exclusively from malted barley in single distilleries that add their distinct character to each whisky label. Like a fine wine bottled at a great chateau, the world-renowned classic single malts (pictured on page 140) are a product of their environment, based on the skill of the individual distiller.

The rest of the world is catching on to the culinary benefits of Scotch whisky. Scotch may be used to deglaze a pan as you would use wine, but it also goes well in sauces and makes a great base for a marinade. Cakes can be soaked in Scotch and fruit salads can be drenched in a mixture of honey, Scotch, and cream. Remember that Scotch is a hardy spirit. Its flavor creates a stronger effect than cooking with wine, beer or brandy. Just one or two tablespoons can make a very big difference. Either blended or single-malt Scotch may be used in cooking.

A salmon marinated in whisky and served with a horseradish salsa, is one of the many recipes using single-malt whiskies. These classic single malts are recommended by Gleneagles Chef Alan Hill: Glenkinchie, Talisker, Dalwhinnie, Oban, Cragganmore, and Lagavulin.

But the latter, because it is more expensive and more distinctive in flavor, also makes a nice accompaniment to a meal or can be served as an apéritif.

The general rule of thumb when cooking with whisky, according to Chef Alan Hill, is that the heartier or more "rustic" the food, the stronger the peat flavor should be in the single malt you choose. For the classic single malts or their substitutes, choose the *Glenkinchie* for poultry and soups. This malt begins in the Lowlands where the surrounding grassy banks keep the whisky soft, restrained, and slightly sweet. *Dalwhinnie* is great with desserts as it has a light, aromatic, and fruity flavor from the snowbound hills of the Highlands. *Cragganmore* is great with poultry and lighter game meats as its origins are in the forests, so it produces a more robust flavor. *Oban*, also from the Highlands, is recommended for cooking with lamb as it offers a peaty, rugged flavor. Seafood is great cooked with *Talisker* with origins in sea lochs. Lashed by winds around a rocky coastline, the *Lagavulin* whisky complements red meats and game as its tang of the sea and the earth is deep with peat.

Once you have tried cooking with Scotch, it may no longer be a novelty and you will move some from the spirits pantry by the home bar to the spices-and-flavorings cupboard in the kitchen, placing the grain next to the grape in perfect harmony.

For more recipes using Scotch whisky, see index. ◆

Whisky and Herb-Marinated Salmon with Horseradish Salsa

The horseradish salsa tames this salmon marinated in whisky. The dish also incorporates a creamy potato salad that is worth keeping in your recipe files.

Salmon:
- 8 ounces smoked salmon filet, cut into medallions
- 1/4 cup single-malt whisky, such as Cardhu
- 1/2 teaspoon sugar
  Sprinkling of fresh dill and tarragon

Potato Salad:
- 2 pounds white potatoes, peeled, cooked, cooled, and sliced into 1/4-inch-thick slices
- 1/4 cup chopped shallots
- 1 garlic clove, finely minced
  Salt and freshly ground pepper
- 1 tablespoon grated horseradish
- 3/4 cup crème fraîche
- 1 teaspoon chopped parsley
- 1/8 teaspoon grated nutmeg

Salsa:
- 4 egg yolks
- 2 tablespoons white wine
- 2 tablespoons creamed horseradish
- 2 tablespoons country-style mustard
- 2 tablespoons olive oil
  Juice of 1 lemon
- 1 tablespoon simple syrup (see page 213)
- 2 tablespoons chopped fresh dill
- 1/8 teaspoon cayenne pepper

Assembly:
- 2 cups or more green-leaf lettuce
- 2 tablespoons walnut oil

Marinate the salmon for 1 hour in the refrigerator in a mixture of the whisky, sugar, and herbs. Turn frequently.

Place the potatoes in a large bowl. Add the remaining ingredients and mix well. Refrigerate and prepare the salsa. (You may sauté the salmon in 2 tablespoons of butter, as another alternative.)

Mix together the egg yolks and white wine over hot (not boiling) water sabayon style or over a double boiler. The end result should be a thick, frothy mixture, done without curdling the eggs. Add the horseradish and mustard. Whisk in the olive oil, lemon, and simple syrup. Add the dill. Season with salt and freshly ground pepper and cayenne. Set aside.

Coat the lettuce with the walnut oil. Place the salmon medallions in the center of the serving plates. Surround with the lettuce. Place the potato salad in the center. Pour the salsa overtop and serve immediately. (Add some of the marinade if desired.) Yield: 4 appetizer servings. ◆

An ancient wine press on Crete, said to be the world's oldest

The Temple of Poseidon
in Sounion

GREECE

Cooking in the Shadow of the Parthenon

Chef Stavroula Paparouna

SYMPOSIO RESTAURANT, ATHENS

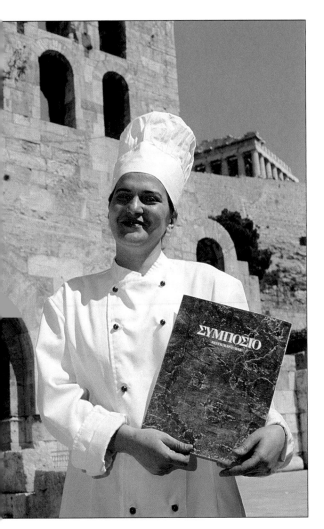

It was 440 B.C. when stone columns arose on the highest hill above a valley of farms. Today, the columns at the Acropolis rise again as stonemasons repair crumbling structures in the manner of their ancestors.

Just below, another tradition continues — eating, feasting, and discussing the concerns of the day. The Symposio is aptly named, for twenty-four hundred years ago — straight up from the restaurant, at that same hill that hosts the ancient Parthenon — Athenians ate, drank, and philosophized about their times. In old Greek, they called this gathering a *symposia.*

Coming here every day since 1987, Chef Paparouna no longer takes much note of her famous venue. Cooking is on her mind as it has been since she watched her mother in the kitchen. "I was fascinated by how she could change an ingredient into something completely different — how she could make a potato or an orange into a thing of beauty and wonderful taste," explains the chef.

When it was time to make a career decision, Chef Paparouna attended culinary school for two years and was soon hired by Symposio. The chef's métier is incorporating traditional Greek ingredients in new ways. The Shrimp with Dill and Ouzo, for example, marries traditional Greek ingredients with a French-inspired sauce. And you will also find plenty of salmon in savory creams and foie gras on the menu.

Guests at the restaurant dine on white china that is Chef Paparouna's porcelain palette. Her fabric canvas receives strokes from a real brush as she paints in the modern medium in her spare time. Her dishes at tableside, with their contemporary designs done in splashes of herbs and dabs of colorful sauces, are in delightful contrast to the more subdued time period of the restaurant. The Symposio building was the Victorian home of a Greek general. It boasts ceiling medallions and soft pink walls with aqua trim and ornate, creamy plaster borders.

In warmer weather, a winter greenhouse dining room opens up to the warm night air. Conversations and compliments to the chef can be heard from diners who marvel at the shimmer of warm lights or the music from a classical concert that may be sounding gently in the ancient amphitheatre just above them. The *symposia* or *Symposio* is the same — only the faces have changed, reflecting broad smiles after a satisfying meal from Chef Paparouna. ◆

> "
> *I was fascinated by how she could change an ingredient into something completely different.*
> "

CHEF STAVROULA PAPAROUNA

Baked Spaghetti and Beef with Cheese Sauce

Known as pastítsio in Greece, this very popular dish is great for a family dinner or for a buffet.

Filling:

3	tablespoons olive oil
1	pound chopped beef (hamburger meat)
1	medium onion, diced
1	clove garlic, chopped
3	medium, ripe tomatoes, blanched, peeled, and chopped
1	cup water
1	small bunch parsley, chopped
	Salt and pepper
1	pound spaghetti #4

Cheese Sauce:

3	tablespoons butter
3	tablespoons all-purpose flour
4	cups hot milk
	Salt and pepper
$^1/_8$	teaspoon nutmeg
1	egg, slightly beaten
1	cup Parmesan cheese

In a large skillet, heat the olive oil and begin to sauté the beef. When the meat is no longer pink, add the onion and garlic and continue sautéing until the meat begins to brown. Add the tomatoes, water, and parsley, and stir well. Add salt and pepper to taste. Continue to cook the mixture over medium-high heat until all of the liquid evaporates (about 40 minutes).

As the meat is cooking, boil the pasta until al dente. Drain, run through cool water, set aside.

continued on page 147

Shrimp with Dill and Ouzo, and pastítsio across from the Acropolis

Meanwhile, preheat the oven to 350° and prepare the cheese sauce. In a small saucepan, melt the butter over medium heat. Add the flour and stir until the flour dissolves completely. Add hot milk gradually. Add the salt and pepper to taste and the nutmeg.

Bring the sauce to a boil and add 2 tablespoons of this to the egg. Return egg mixture to the pot. Stir well. Add the cheese and stir until melted. Grease a 9x13-inch baking dish. Line the bottom of the pan with the spaghetti. Add the meat and tomato filling. Cover with the cheese sauce. Bake for 20 to 30 minutes or until the crust turns a golden brown. Yield: 4-6 servings. ◆

Shrimp with Dill and Ouzo

The national drink of Greece is ouzo, an anise-tasting/liqueur-style beverage that is also used prolifically in cooking. In this rendition from the Symposio restaurant, the chef offers a refreshing recipe that makes a wonderful appetizer or main course, and it's a cinch to prepare.

1	tablespoon olive oil
20	large shrimp, cleaned and deveined
½	cup ouzo
2	medium tomatoes, blanched, peeled, seeded, and chopped
3	finely chopped tablespoons fresh dill
½	cup heavy cream
	Salt and pepper

Heat the oil in a large skillet. Add the shrimp and sauté about 2 minutes. Pour in the ouzo; add the tomatoes and dill and boil for about 3 minutes. Add the heavy cream and stir well. Season with salt and pepper to taste. Allow to boil for 3 minutes. Serve immediately. Yield: 4 main servings. ◆

Wine Suggestion

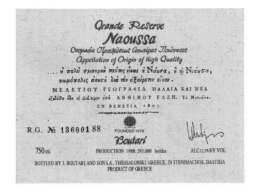

From the birthplace of Dionysos, God of Wine, comes the richly textured **Boutari Grand Reserve Naoussa.** Made from Xinomavro grapes and barrel-aged in oak, this full-bodied, dry red wine perfectly accompanies the hearty pastítsio.

Wine Suggestion

The flavorful, full-bodied **Kourtaki Vin de Crete** dry white wine with its aromatic hint of green apple, accents seafood, such as Chef Paparouna's Shrimp with Dill and Ouzo. The wine is made from Vilana grapes, grown only on Crete.

...As Busy as a Bee as the World Drops By

Chef Athanasios Apostolopoulos

HOTEL AMALIA, DELPHI

"Greeks eat honey like bears," or so the expression goes with those who know Greek eating habits. Whether enjoying honey right off a spoon, mixing it with plain, whipped yogurt and nuts, or incorporating it into a pot on the stove and a pan in the oven, whenever there's a chance to include honey, Greeks have been doing so since ancient times. Brightly painted hives dot the Greek countryside where bees feast at flowers and herbs.

Tucked in the midst of olive trees, off a winding dirt road, Chef Athanasios Apostolopoulos tends to his own cache of beehives, producing honey as a hobby. It seems a fitting complement to his daily job as executive chef at the Amalia Hotel, where honey is brought in by the gallon. You may find him baking the well-known *loukoumades* — bite-size balls of flour and sugar, cooked in pools of fresh honey.

You never really know what Chef Apostolopoulos will be cooking on a given day. The Amalia is a popular hotel with tourists by the busload from all over Europe, who keep the chef busy in his large, family-style dining room. He makes the extra effort to check with the reception desk to find out the predominant nationality of guests staying over for a period of days.

"I then make up a menu, taking into consideration dishes from their own country as well as figuring out ways to adapt Greek dishes or other continental recipes to their palate." In any case, Chef Apostolopoulos likes to pick his ingredients fresh and may be seen as the daily fishing boat pulls in at sunset in nearby Itea, with the day's catch. Everyone from Orthodox priests to private citizens and restaurateurs can be found socializing at the dock, waiting for the boat to land.

With the catch of the day, this chef suggests: rather than sticking to white wine with fish and red wine with meat, "You should choose whatever wine your taste prefers." With that in mind, he recommends white wine with the lighter dishes he prepares and red with the heavier ones. In either case, he believes the wine should be dry or semi-dry.

While the selection of wine is very important in Greece, so is the selection of honey. Connoisseurs of honey, like wine tasters, judge the sweetener by aroma, clarity, and flavor. These factors, as with the grapes that are grown for wine, are determined by the soil where the flowers grow. Since the flavor of honey is mainly determined by the flowers from which bees feed, there are as many types of honey in Greece as there are flowering plants.

Chef Apostolopoulos, hunched over his hives, is happy to be contributing to honey production in Greece. As someone once said, "How sweet it is." ◆

Grilled Eggplant Salad and Baked Stuffed Vegetables with Pignoli Nuts and Raisins bow before the Treasury of Athens at Delphi. Recipe for Tiropita (cheese pies at far left) is on page 169.

Grilled Eggplant Salad

Eggplant is an extremely popular ingredient in Greek cookery, and this recipe offers a creative way to prepare the vegetable. Called *Melitzanosalata* in Greek, serve this as a salad with dinner; as a luncheon plate; or as an appetizer spread on pita, French bread, or crackers. This recipe calls for grilling over an open fire, such as a charcoal cooker, but you may also use an oven broiler (see end of recipe). Although very simple to prepare, you will need to start this recipe 24 hours in advance.

2   medium, long and slim eggplants
     (about 1 1/4 pounds each)
2   tablespoons white or red wine vinegar
     Juice of 2 lemons
1   tablespoon extra virgin olive oil
1   tablespoon vegetable oil
2   tablespoons chopped onion
1   large garlic clove, mashed
1/2   teaspoon sugar
1/4   teaspoon salt
1/8   teaspoon black pepper
     Flat-leaf parsley, chopped, for garnish

continued on page 151

A volcanic eruption in 1500 B.C. shaped the magnificent Greek island of Santorini into the form of a crescent moon. Today, vineyards here produce the grapes for Boutari Santorini, the wine recommended as a complement to the chef's Grilled Eggplant Salad.

Using the tines of a fork, pierce the eggplants with tiny holes to prevent them from exploding during grilling. If you are using a charcoal grill, the holes will also allow the smoky flavor to be absorbed into the vegetable. Place the eggplants on the grill 3 to 4 inches above medium-hot coals. Grill, turning occasionally for about 30 minutes or until the eggplants are evenly charred and soft. (They will just begin to collapse.) Remove to a platter.

When cool enough to handle, remove the stems and charred skin. Place the eggplants in a colander set over a deep bowl. Cover with plastic wrap and allow them to drain in the refrigerator for about 24 hours.

Place the drained eggplants on a work surface and cut in half lengthwise. Spread open the sections of the eggplant halves and remove as many of the seeds as possible. Chop the eggplant finely and place in a medium bowl. Set aside.

In another bowl, mix together all of the other ingredients except the parsley. Pour the mixture into the chopped eggplant and gently combine.

Cover and chill for a few hours before serving to allow the salad to marinate. Yield: 6 appetizer servings. ◆

NOTE: *To broil in an oven, preheat the broiler. Place the punctured eggplants on a rack 6 to 8 inches below the heat source. Broil, turning occasionally until the eggplants are charred all over, soft, and starting to collapse.*

Wine Suggestion

SANTORINI

ΟΝΟΜΑΣΙΑ ΠΡΟΕΛΕΥΣΕΩΣ ΑΝΩΤΕΡΑΣ ΠΟΙΟΤΗΤΟΣ
APPELLATION OF ORIGIN OF HIGH QUALITY
WHITE WINE
1993

Net Cont. 750 ml   BOUTARI   Alc. 12, 5 % by Vol.

BOTTLED BY:
J. BOUTARI AND SON S.A., THESSALONIKI, GREECE, IN STENIMACHOS, IMATHIA.
Ελληνικό προϊόν

The delicate, dry white **Boutari Santorini** is made from grapes grown on the island of Santorini, considered by some to be the remains of the lost continent of Atlantis. Citrus overtones balance the smokiness of the grilled eggplant.

Baked Stuffed Vegetables with Pignoli Nuts and Raisins

An interesting mix of spices and other ingredients fills this nutritional recipe that may be served as an appetizer or main course (see photo page 149). Use the small-sized vegetables if serving as an appetizer.

═══════════════

8	small or 4 large, ripe tomatoes
1/2	tablespoon sugar
	Sea salt to taste
8	small or 4 large green bell peppers
4	medium eggplants
1/2	cup extra virgin olive oil, plus 2 tablespoons
3	medium onions, grated
1	teaspoon ground allspice
1	teaspoon freshly ground black pepper
2 1/2	cups long-grain rice, cooked
3/4	cup lightly toasted pignoli nuts
1	tablespoon oregano, crumbled
1/2	cup dark raisins or currants
1/2	cup finely chopped flat-leaf parsley
2	tablespoons tomato paste
	Juice of 1 lemon
1/2	cup fresh, whole-wheat breadcrumbs
1	cup water
	Lemon wedges

═══════════════

Preheat the oven to 325°. Slice off the tops of the tomatoes. Scoop out the pulp with a small spoon. Discard the seeds and dice the pulp. Set aside with their juices. Sprinkle the sugar and salt into the tomato shells. Invert onto a paper towel and set aside to drain.

Slice off the tops of the peppers. Discard the cores and remove the seeds. Trim the stems off the eggplants. Cut them in half lengthwise. Heat 2

continued on page 152

tablespoons of the olive oil in a medium skillet and fry the eggplants until they turn golden brown and the skin darkens and wrinkles. Remove from the pan and drain on a paper towel. When cooled enough to handle, scoop out the flesh with a small spoon. Discard the seeds and dice the pulp.

In a heavy skillet, heat 1/4 cup of the olive oil and sauté the onion over low heat until golden brown, stirring occasionally. Add the reserved tomato dice and juices, diced eggplant pulp, allspice, pepper, and about 1 teaspoon salt. Cook 5 minutes or until most of the liquid has evaporated. Using a fork, stir in the rice, pignoli nuts, oregano, raisins, and half the parsley. Season to taste. Stir in the tomato paste. Remove from the heat.

Arrange the vegetables in a baking dish, stuffing each with the filling evenly divided. Sprinkle the lemon juice and 1/4 cup of olive oil overtop. Sprinkle the breadcrumbs over the tomatoes only.

Add the water and 2 tablespoons olive oil to the bottom of the dish and bake 1 hour or until the vegetables are tender, basting frequently with the liquid in the pan. Add a little more water to the pan if it appears to be drying out.

To serve, arrange the vegetables on a platter and sprinkle with the pan juices, more olive oil, if desired, and the remaining parsley. Add the lemon wedges for garnish. Yield: 4 servings. ◆

Wine Suggestion

Legend has it that the ruby-red wines of Nemea gave Hercules the strength to slay the lion. **Kouros Nemea's** deep cherry aroma harmonizes with the intricate spices of Chef Apostolopoulos' baked stuffed vegetable dish.

Even the local Orthodox priest turns out for the fish market at Itea's harbor.

Fresh red snapper — shown at seaside Galaxidi near Delphi – is used prolifically by the Amalia chef and throughout the Mediterranean. Marinate the fish in ³/₄ cup each olive oil and lemon juice, ¹/₂ teaspoon dried oregano, and salt and pepper to taste. Bake at 375° for 20 minutes.

Getting Out of Jail with a Recipe...

Chef Stephan DeMichelis

HOTEL PENTELIKON, KIFISSIA

*I*f being an organized chef — from concerns of the table to those of the kitchen office — were a criteria for culinary bravado, Chef Stephan DeMichelis would certainly garner an award. A neat-and-tidy culinary workroom only hints at this chef's sensitivity and dedication to his work. You know that if he acts this way, he thinks this way, and the end result must be in his cooking. And it is.

Perhaps it has something to do with Chef DeMichelis' background as the son of a medical doctor. He began his career in France, washing dishes in the hospital where his father worked. After three months, he began cooking and planning meals — having had enough time to discover his innate talent.

It was on to culinary school and then recognition by some of the top cooks in France. In Nice, he was selected to train with Jacques Chibois and Christian Willer. In Paris, he studied with renowned Swiss chef Fredy Giardet.

Looking through Chef DeMichelis' scrapbook, you can find him pictured with European celebrities and see his name over and over again in articles from local and international culinary newspapers and magazines. He also trained across the Atlantic, and in a short time was cooking for President George Bush.

"Americans need to expand their horizons when it comes to enjoying foods," notes Chef DeMichelis. "Don't get in jail with a recipe," he advises. "Make your own adaptation." Having been a chef for the prestigious Four Seasons hotels, he got a taste of America and liked its flavorings. "My advice is to try at least one thing you have never had before when you go out to dinner," suggests the chef. He hopes that he can help more Americans expand their culinary adventures.

He's doing just that in the Vardis Dining Room at the plush Hotel Pentelikon, located in the upscale suburbs of Athens. The dining room was luxuriously decorated under the watchful eye of hotel owner Harry Vardis. An Italian interior designer did faux painting and effects such as the miles of elegant fabric that cascade from the center of the Vardis room to every inch of the ceiling. Silver plate chargers and Victorian chairs grace the tables — every one with a soothing, romantic view of the hotel's botanical gardens and Grecian stoneware.

The restaurant seats only fifty, "in order to prepare the best quality food and service," explains Vardis, who opened thirty-two other successful restaurants in Australia.

This kind of atmosphere complements the pristine way Chef DeMichelis works behind the scenes. And as his beautifully arranged dishes make their way to the tables, the circle of perfection from decor to atmosphere to exquisite food — is complete. ◆

Classical details form the backdrop for the Lobster Youvetsi on the luxurious grounds of the hotel.

Lobster Youvetsi

Usually, when a menu item or a recipe has the word *youvetsi* in it, you can count on the fact that the dish will be made en casserole with meat, pasta, and vegetables.

The most common youvetsi is a lamb made with orzo pasta, but Chef DeMichelis adds a new twist to this version. First of all, he uses lobster and then he bakes it in a small, individual crock with dough that forms a crusty topping — something like a pot pie, only this bakes with the lid on top, allowing the dough to spill out, forming a crust.

Youvetsi comes from the Turkish *youvets,* meaning cooked casserole-style.

Concassée:
- 4 *large, ripe tomatoes, blanched, skinned, and seeded*
  Olive oil
- 1 *shallot, chopped*
- 1/8 *teaspoon sugar*
- 1 *clove garlic*
- 2 *tablespoons fresh rosemary*

Pasta and Lobster:
- 2 *pounds lobster meat*
- 2 *cloves garlic*
- 1 *branch rosemary*
- 1/2 *pound penne pasta*
- 2 *cups lobster or fish stock*
- 1/2 *cup chopped truffles or mushrooms*
  Fresh basil
  Olive oil
  Salt and pepper

Crust:
- 1 *cup all-purpose flour*
- 3 *tablespoons butter*
- 2 *egg yolks*
- 1 *teaspoon white vinegar*
- 1/8 *teaspoon salt*

Prepare the tomatoes concassée style. Blanch the tomatoes, peel them, and remove the seeds. In a medium skillet, heat 2 tablespoons olive oil. Add the shallot and sauté for 2 minutes. Add the tomatoes, sugar, garlic, and rosemary, and cook on medium heat for about 10 minutes. Set a large stockpot to boil with enough water to cover lobster. Add 2 tablespoons olive oil, 2 cloves garlic, 1 branch rosemary. Boil for 20 minutes. Remove lobster. Cool, clean, and cut into chunks. Reserve 2 cups of lobster stock.

Meanwhile, prepare the dough. In a large mixing bowl, mix together the flour, butter, 1 of the egg yolks, the vinegar, and salt. Form the dough into a ball and roll out to about 1/8-inch thickness. Cover. Set aside.

Just before the concasseé is finished, cook the pasta in boiling water until al dente. Drain and assemble the casserole.

Preheat the oven to 350°. Using individual ramekins or baking dishes with lids (about 6 inches round), evenly divide the concassée and the pasta into the dish. Add the lobster, lobster stock, and truffles, along with a sprinkling of fresh basil, olive oil, and salt and pepper to taste.

Brush remaining egg yolk on rim of baking dish. Press a portion of dough along the edge of each dish. Add the lid.

Brush with egg yolk. Bake for at least 15 minutes or until the crust turns golden brown. (If necessary, remove the lid and bake 5 minutes more to attain a golden brown color overall.) Serve either in the baking dish, or turn out onto a dinner plate. Yield: 4 servings. ◆

Wine Suggestion

The berry-like flavors of the dry, red **Kourtaki Vin de Crete** make an interesting accompaniment to hearty seafood dishes such as the Lobster Youvetsi.

Octopus with Lemon Sauce

Octopus is a popular dish in Greece, especially in summertime when the aroma of the grilling seafood permeates seaside *tavernas*. When octopuses are caught, they are pounded on rocks to help tenderize them. They are then dried in the sun before grilling. This dish is easy to prepare and makes an interesting appetizer. Prepare this dish a day ahead of time.

2   small green bell peppers
2   large red bell peppers
    Juice of 2 lemons
    Salt
5   tablespoons olive oil
1   tablespoon each chopped fresh oregano and
    rosemary
1   octopus (about 2 pounds, fresh or frozen)
1   cup dry white wine
2   lemons for garnish

Roast the bell peppers until their skins are charred and blackened on the outside (see method, page 209). Remove the skins and cut the peppers into a small dice. In another bowl, whisk together the lemon juice, salt, chopped and roasted peppers, olive oil, oregano, and rosemary. Set aside.

Prepare the octopus. On the day before, remove the eyes, mouth, and insides of head. Rinse well. Place in a large saucepan with 1 cup wine. Add water to cover. Bring to a slow boil. Cover. Reduce heat. Simmer 45 minutes. Rinse. Store in covered container in refrigerator overnight. Day of serving, peel off skin to reveal pink flesh. Boil the whole octopus for about 20 minutes in salted water. Remove the octopus from the water and cook it on the grill for 5 minutes on each side until a fork easily pierces it. Cut off each of the tentacles.

To serve, pour the lemon sauce onto the individual serving plates. Add lemon slices for garnish, if desired. Yield: 6 appetizer servings. ◆

Wine Suggestion

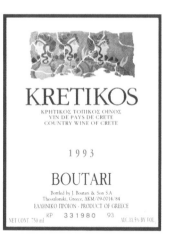

Sweet aromas of orange flowers in the **Boutari Kretikos** make a wonderful counterpoint to the lemon sauce in Chef DeMichelis' grilled octopus.

Grilled octopus is a favorite at the Pentelikon and all over Greece.

Bungalows by the Bay and Cretan Village Dining

Chef George Niòtis

ELOUNDA BEACH HOTEL, CRETE

*S*porting a sense of humor and a zest for food, it quickly becomes apparent that Chef George Niòtis loves the cooking life. He has been at it ever since he first realized: "I love to eat good things and knew I would have to cook them to enjoy them."

That's what brought him to Elounda Beach. This exclusive resort draws Greek dignitaries to Crete, the largest of Greece's two-thousand-plus islands and easily reached by air and sea from Athens. One of the hotel's notable visitors is the country's prime minister, who had his own villa built on the premises.

Whether statesman or not, guests feel special at Elounda Beach. Stone villas, or bungalows as they are called by the hotel, have their own private waterfronts overlooking Mirabello Bay. Each bungalow has a stone veranda and steps to a patio at water's edge. The hotel took its cue from the surrounding landscape, matching the stones in the old walls along the mountainsides where farmers keep their goats within view.

Included on the hotel's grounds is a small village that contains a Cretan museum with culinary artifacts and a weaver's shop where doilies, pillows, and other assorted fabric accents are woven for the hotel. There are clothing and gift boutiques, a *taverna* where *mezedes* are served with a glass of ouzo, and a whitewashed Orthodox Catholic church with typical Greek sky-blue roof and a frescoe-lined interior.

The hotel's flagship dining room, Dionysos, is the focal point of the village. Flickering lights from antique lanterns invite diners to sit outdoors. Always "docked" just outside the restaurant is a brightly painted, old blue-and-white boat, overflowing with Greek ingredients under glass that hint at what's in the chef's specials. Inside, guests enjoy candlelight and a slow, blazing fire on cool evenings.

Although Chef Niòtis creates international cuisine here, Greek gourmet specialties are also sought after, such as the tasty and delicate recipe for squid. "Greek food is becoming fashionable," he says, "because the world is recognizing how healthy it is."

The chef's venue at Elounda Beach is a pampering one. Every effort is made to keep this sprawling resort casually elegant with a personal presence. In another dining room at the main hotel, folk art paintings (on old trunk lids) hang on the walls as part of the owner's personal collection of Cretan art. And the hotel's logo of a merry mermaid is found floating on stationery, paperweights, and as stencils on glass patio doors, reminding every visiting mermaid or merman to make the visit to Elounda Beach a fabled one. ◆

Time out for tea, Kataifi (the stringy sweet), and a letter home

Greek food is becoming fashionable because the world is recognizing how healthy it is.

CHEF GEORGE NIÒTIS

Kataifi with Almonds

A bit like the famous baklava, Kataifi — or shredded dough — is a mainstay of the Greek dessert cart, and it's easy to make. A ubiquitous ingredient of Greek desserts, honey in this country is generally darker and thicker than that produced in other parts of the world. Kataifi is a very thin, dry dough that resembles capelli d'angelo (angel hair) spaghetti, but it's even lighter and is available through Greek suppliers (see Resource Directory).

Dough:

1	cup butter, melted
1	pound kataifi, strands separated
1	cup shelled almonds, finely chopped
1	tablespoon grated lemon peel
$^1/_2$	teaspoon cinnamon

Syrup:

1 ½   cups sugar
1 ½   cups water
1   cup quality thick honey
1   tablespoon lemon juice

Preheat the oven to 400°. Pour ½ cup of the melted butter into a 9x13-inch glass baking dish. Separate the kataifi dough into shreds. Sprinkle half of the shreds over the butter in the baking dish, pressing them down lightly with the palm of your hand.

In a small bowl, combine the almonds, lemon peel, and cinnamon. Sprinkle evenly over the kataifi. Sprinkle the remaining kataifi over the nut mixture, pressing down as before.

Drizzle with the remaining half cup butter and bake 25 to 35 minutes or until golden brown.

While the kataifi is baking, combine the sugar, water, honey, and lemon juice in a small saucepan over high heat. Bring to a boil, stirring constantly with a wooden spoon until the sugar is dissolved. Boil for 5 minutes. Set aside to cool slightly.

Remove the kataifi from the oven and set aside to cool on a wire rack for about 10 minutes. Pour the very warm syrup over the kataifi. Cut into squares or rectangles to serve. Yield: 10-12 servings. ◆

Spirit Suggestion

The mellow taste of the brandy-like spirit **Metaxa Seven Star** makes it an ideal accompaniment to the honey-sweet Kataifi.

Baked Tomato-and-Rice-Stuffed Squid

At Elounda Beach, they make this dish with cuttlefish, a Mediterranean favorite. But cuttlefish is harder to find in other parts of the world, so substitute with squid, a related mollusk also known as calamari. Calamari and cuttlefish are very popular Greek dishes, and stuffing them is one of the most common forms of preparation.

¼   cup olive oil
1   medium white onion, chopped
3   scallions, chopped
    Tentacles from 2 squid or cuttlefish, chopped
2   tablespoons uncooked, long-grain rice
2   large, ripe tomatoes, blanched, seeded, peeled, and chopped, plus 2 tomato slices for garnish
1   cup white wine
    Salt and pepper
1   teaspoon finely chopped parsley, plus more for garnish
1   teaspoon dried oregano
2   whole and cleaned squid (about 6 ounces each)
½   cup water

Heat a 1-quart saucepan filled with water. Meanwhile, in a deep skillet, heat 2 tablespoons of the olive oil over low heat. Add the white onion and cook about 1 minute. Stir in the scallions and the squid tentacles. Immediately add the rice and sauté, stirring constantly to prevent the rice from sticking. Add the tomatoes (except the garnish) and stir in the wine. Add salt and pepper to taste. Stir the mixture over the heat until the rice is tender and the mixture thickens, about 20 minutes. Remove from the heat and stir in the parsley and oregano.

When the hot water has come to a boil, add the squid and cook only until they swell and soften, about 3 minutes. Remove from the water and let cool

continued on page 162

to the touch. Clean pouch of any material. Rinse and pat dry.

Preheat the oven to 350°. Stuff the squid with the tomato-and-rice mixture and place them in a small baking dish. Add 2 tablespoons of oil to the bottom of the pan, along with the $^1/_2$ cup of water. Sprinkle salt and pepper overtop the squid. Bake for 10 minutes or until the stuffing is heated through. Garnish with a tomato slice and chopped parsley. Yield: 2 servings. ◆

Wine Suggestion

Lac des Roches
DRY WHITE TABLE WINE

boutari
Founded 1879

Net Cont. 750 ml

BOTTLED BY J. BOUTARI AND SON SA.
THESSALONIKI, GREECE A.K.M./09-0014/84
PRODUCT OF GREECE

Alc. 11.5% by vol.

The delicate grapefruit aroma of the **Boutari Lac des Roches** perfectly contrasts the very tasty Baked Tomato-and-Rice-Stuffed Squid.

Sweeping arches of an Elounda Beach bungalow frame the stuffed squid and Mirabello Bay.

An Athenian Legend Hosts the World

Chef Jacky Froger

HOTEL GRANDE BRETAGNE, ATHENS

The G.B. Corner restaurant at the Hotel Grande Bretagne is decidedly elegant but with the whimsical spirit of a British café, seemingly out of place in the midst of ancient Greek surroundings. The Grande Bretagne is a short walk from the Plaka — an old Greek community with whitewashed neoclassical buildings, stone steps, ornate little churches, potted geraniums, and wrought-iron balconies.

But the hotel does fit in well with its modern environment and its link to the past. Its roots are in the nineteenth century when wealthy English travelers used the hotel as a stopover enroute to the antiquities of Egypt. Thus, the Grande Bretagne — or Great Britain — was named in their honor. Today, this legendary hotel hosts the world. Across the street at the Greek Parliament building, guards in colorful skirted *evzones* stand sentinel until they change posts, then it's legs and arms up in marching cadence.

The very British heritage is the backdrop for Chef Jacky Froger, whose roots are neither here in Greece nor there in England, but in his native France. Only his heart is in Greece where he found his wife of twenty-two years. Jacky's background, which includes working on cruise ships that sail the Mediterranean, has given his decidedly French style of cooking a flair for the continental.

Greek specialties served at G.B. Corner range from moussaka made gratin-style with eggplant, meat, and cheese to an *arnaki lemonato* or baby lamb in lemon sauce with rice.

The pleasant contrast greets diners as they sit at dark-leather booths marked by wooden pub signs made by local Greek artists. Reproduction gas lanterns light the booths that are divided by smoky, etched glass. Pink linen napkins bear the hotel logo. Elegant touches are everywhere and harken back to the days when the hotel was a private mansion, built in 1862 by a wealthy Athenian. The mansion was later turned into a French archaeological school until it was purchased and made into a hotel.

Today's guests at the restaurant seek Chef Froger's primarily French-prepared dishes. For *World Class Cuisine,* the chef showed us how to spice up a dish with Greek ingredients.

The shrimp with Feta cheese utilizes Greek's most popular cheese. Feta cheese is used prolifically in Greek cooking because of its tremendous versatility. Feta has a sublime flavor that can either balance the spices in a recipe or be served alone with spices added. We can thank Chef Froger for combining the traditions that surround his workplace to make such a special recipe. ◆

Changing of the guard at the Greek Parliament across the street from the Grande Bretagne

Vegetarian Stuffed Grape Leaves with Yogurt

Also known as vine leaves, grape leaves are sturdy but edible wrappers for a variety of stuffings. Here, Chef Froger prepares his own version of this classic Greek dish. Grape leaves are a healthy, dark-leaf vegetable that may also be shredded into salads, and they make great garnishes.

1	pound grape leaves, preserved in brine
3/4	cup pure olive oil
3	medium onions, finely chopped
3	cups long-grain rice
2	tablespoons finely chopped, flat-leaf parsley
3	tablespoons finely chopped dill
	Salt and pepper to taste
1 1/2	cups warm water
1/2	cup fresh lemon juice
1	cup plain yogurt, for garnish

Using plenty of hot water, *thoroughly* rinse the brine from the preserved grape leaves. Drain and set aside.

In a large heavy skillet, heat the oil and sauté the onions until translucent. Add the rice, parsley, dill, salt, pepper, and warm water. Cook this mixture half-covered over low heat for about 10 minutes, stirring occasionally, until the rice is half cooked and no liquid remains in the skillet.

To fill the grape leaves, place them flat on a work surface, shiny side down. Remove the tough stems. Spoon some of the rice mixture onto the widest part of each leaf. Fold up the bottom of the leaf and then the sides. Roll up towards the tip.

Spread a few of the larger, unstuffed leaves on the bottom of a large saucepan. Tightly pack the stuffed leaves on top of that, folded side down, to keep them from unwrapping. Press a heatproof plate

Vegetarian Stuffed Grape Leaves with Yogurt at a peaceful square in the historic Plaka section of Athens

> *Feta cheese is used prolifically in Greek cooking because of its tremendous versatility. Feta has a sublime flavor that can either balance the spices in a recipe or be served alone with spices added.*

Wine Suggestion

The deep, ruby red, velvet-textured **Boutari Paros** balances the tart taste of the delightful grape leaves dish from the Grande Bretagne.

down on top of them so that they do not move while cooking. Add enough hot water to cover the leaves. Add the lemon juice. Simmer the leaves, covered for about 1 hour or until they are tender and the rice is well cooked. Serve warm or cold. Add dollops of yogurt as a garnish. Yield: 12-14 appetizer servings. ◆

Shrimp with Tomato and Feta Cheese en Cocotte

A recipe that bears the term *cocotte* as part of its title signals that this dish will cook slowly in a round or oval glass, ceramic, enamel, or stainless steel pan. In this delicious rendition, Chef Froger prepares this combination of Greek ingredients with a French touch, in individual ovenproof dishes. It is easy to prepare and is great as an appetizer or main course.

1   tablespoon tomato paste
$^1\!/_2$ cup dry white wine
$^3\!/_4$ cup olive oil
1   large onion, diced
1   large carrot, diced
2   tablespoons celery, diced
4   ripe tomatoes, blanched, skinned, seeded, and finely chopped, concassée style (see page 209)
1   teaspoon honey
2   pounds shelled but uncooked shrimp or prawns
1   pound soft (not too salty) Feta cheese, crumbled
   Salt and pepper

Begin by making a tomato sauce. In a small bowl, dilute the tomato paste in the white wine. Set aside. In a medium saucepan, heat 1 tablespoon of the olive oil. Add the onion and sauté for about 1 minute until it sweats. Add the carrot, celery, tomato concassée, honey, and the tomato paste with wine.

Cook over medium heat for $^1\!/_2$ hour or until the vegetables are soft.

When the sauce is cooked, pour it through a sieve and spread evenly into 8 dishes.

Preheat the oven to 350°. In a medium skillet, heat the remaining olive oil. Add the shrimp and sauté for 5 to 6 minutes. They will be pink in color. Place the shrimp evenly into the tomato sauce in each dish.

Crumbled Feta cheese should be sprinkled into the bed of shrimp, filling nooks and crannies. Bake for 15 minutes or until the dish is piping hot. Yield: 8 appetizer servings. ◆

Wine Suggestion

To woo Cleopatra, legend says that Caesar served her fine white wine from Patras. **Kouros Patras'** crisp, clean taste and lemon-lime flavors heighten seafood dishes such as the Shrimp with Tomato and Feta Cheese en Cocotte.

The ruins of an ancient Athens prison and Shrimp with Tomato and Feta Cheese en Cocotte

Little Meals
The Story of the Greek Meze

*P*erhaps it was Plato who first wrote about the pleasures of the *meze* or the Greek appetizer table. Some twenty-four hundred years ago, he described a spread of many foods. There were cheeses and figs, he suggested, myrtle and olives, radishes and beans, and much more.

After all these years, the tradition continues with the *meze* more popular than ever. The Greeks are passionate about taking leisure time to enjoy their *mezedes* that are brought to the table on small plates. Tidbits of fresh and preserved delicacies, meats, seafoods, vegetables,

Olive groves stretch from the sea to the mountains in Itea.

condiments, and always loaves of crusty country breads are festively passed around the table. There is a seemingly endless number of these little dishes that, instead of being hors d'oeuvres, become the meal itself.

fact, even young Greeks find this way of entertaining to be pleasant and lively. Preparing so many different little meals is somewhat time-consuming. But because many appetizers may be made months in advance and pickled, and many more may be bought (see Krinos Foods in Resource Directory), it is often the easiest way to have a party. The *mezedes* are served and everyone digs in — always enjoying their appetizers with a glass of ouzo, traditional retsina, or a quality white or red wine.

You can serve your own Greek *meze* table at home by cooking up some of the savory dishes offered here. Just make sure you cut pieces bite-size and serve them on small plates. Fill in by purchasing quality Greek condiments; a variety of olives, including green ones stuffed with almonds; and an assortment of Greek cheeses, such as Feta, Kasseri, and Manouri.

Where They Eat Meze

Mezedes are served at *ouzeries* or bars. Romantic *tavernas* also host fresh and plentiful *mezedes* with twenty-five or more dishes served at once. The line of hungry patrons waiting to get in can mean as much as an hour's wait.

The *meze* table is also served at home. In

What's on the Appetizer Table

The *meze* table is a way to become acquainted with Greek food quickly. The photo on page 170 was taken at the Kalathakis Taverna at Knossos on the island of Crete. No one minds waiting in the queue that often forms there. On the table are some 36 little meals from lamb fricassee, moussaka, beans with carrots, and snails with yeast and milk to roasted red pepper, pork with mushrooms in white wine, squid, and cheese pie. Most *meze* tables include bowls of olives and slabs of fresh Feta cheese. The recipes that follow are just a few for your *meze* table. Mix them with other recipes in the Greek section, using small portions.

The creative taverna owner takes care to provide his or her guests with variety, color, texture, and imagination in presenting the assortment of *mezedes*. Flavor and aroma are also essential, but what really has made this custom transcend the ages is people getting together symposia-style for the sake of leisure, merriment, and good company. For Grecians, the *meze* table is reason enough to be Greek, and they don't mind sharing their tradition with the world. Many restaurants in Greece have put their native dishes aside and gone continental. But one thing none seem to give up is their *meze*. Philosopher Plato, of course, must have known it would be this way! ◆

> 66
> *My advice is to try at least one thing you have never had before when you go out to dinner.*
> 99
>
> CHEF STEPHAN DEMICHELIS

Three-Cheese Mini-Pies

In Greece, these delectable, triangular and flaky phyllo pockets are called *tiropita* and they make excellent *meze* items. The Graviera cheese has a sweet, nutty flavor. This recipe was prepared for the *World Class Cuisine* television series by Chef Athanasios Apostolopoulos.

---

1 1/2 cups Feta cheese, crumbled
1   cup small-curd cottage cheese
2   tablespoons grated Graviera or Gruyère cheese
1/4 cup all-purpose flour
2   eggs
1/4 teaspoon white pepper
1   package phyllo dough, thawed (28 leaves)
2   cups butter, melted

In a medium bowl, stir together the cheeses and the flour. In another bowl, beat the eggs with the pepper. Add to the cheese mixture, stirring until blended.

Remove 24 phyllo leaves from the package (saving 4 in case of tearing and re-packaging, and freezing the rest).

Put the sheets so that the longest side is facing you on a large work surface. Using a ruler and a pizza cutter or the tip of a sharp knife, cut the phyllo into 3 strips 5 1/2 inches wide. Take 12 of the strips and fold in half crosswise. Cut at the fold to make 24 pieces. Fold in half again and cut to make 48 rectangles or patches for under the filling. Reserve excess dough for another recipe.

Place 2 strips of pastry on the work surface, short ends facing you. Brush both strips lightly with the butter, starting at the center and working out towards the edges. Place 1 of the rectangular patches crosswise about an inch from the bottom and butter the patch.

Preheat the oven to 350°. Working quickly with 1 strip at a time, place 1 rounded teaspoonful of the filling in the center of the patch. Fold the sides in over the filling. Butter the folds. Starting at the

continued on page 171

Mezedes from the Kalathakis Taverna at Knossos on Crete

bottom, fold into a triangle shape. Continue folding, making sure that with each fold the bottom edge is parallel with the alternate side edge. Lightly butter the finished triangle and place on an ungreased baking sheet. Continue until all of the cheese is used and you have 48 triangles.

Bake in the top third of the oven for 10 minutes. Brush with butter again and continue to bake 10 to 15 minutes or until golden. Remove from the oven and serve immediately or cool on wire racks to be reheated later. Yield: 48 pies. ◆

Spirit Suggestion

The clean licorice flavor of **Ouzo 12** enhances the *meze's* potpourri of spices, herbs, and savory flavors. Magically, ouzo turns cloudy when served over ice.

Stewed Lamb with Romaine Lettuce and Egg-Lemon Sauce

You may have seen this recipe cooked on one of the Elounda Beach *World Class Cuisine* television shows as a main course. But you may also adapt this as a *meze* item by serving smaller portions. Lemon sauces are frequently added to Greek recipes.

Lamb:
- 1 pound boneless leg of lamb, cut into bite-size pieces
- 1/4 cup butter
- 4 scallions, chopped
- 2 tablespoons chopped fresh dill
- 2 cups white wine
- 2 cups water
  Salt and pepper
- 1 medium head romaine lettuce, cut into 1-inch strips

Egg-Lemon Sauce:
- 1 egg yolk
  Juice of 2 lemons
  Juice from the stewed lamb

Place the lamb, butter, scallions, and dill in a wide-mouthed saucepan or stew pan with low (about 3-inch) sides. Sauté on the stovetop over low heat until browned. Add the wine and water and reduce to half over high heat, about 15 minutes. Salt and pepper to taste.

While the lamb stews, blanch the lettuce in boiling water. Add it to the reduced stew and cook for another 15 minutes. Drain the stew juice and set the lamb aside.

Prepare the sauce by whisking together the egg yolk and lemon juice with one hand and diluting the mixture with the other hand by pouring in the lamb stew juice. Heat sauce and then add to the lamb. Yield: 8-10 *meze* servings. ◆

top of the pie five minutes before the recipe is done. Sprinkle the seeds overtop and put back in the oven for the remaining cooking time. The chef's version is made as one whole pie. To serve for the *meze* party, simply cut into bite-size pieces.

Sesame Spinach and Cheese Pie

Known in Greece as *Spanakopitte*, this recipe was cooked on the television series by Chef Stavroula Paparouna of the Symposio restaurant. Like so much Greek food, it is delicious and nutritional and makes a perfect *meze* item.

Some Greeks add a layer of sesame seeds to the

$1/2$ pound fresh spinach, shredded
2   leeks finely chopped, white part only
4   scallions, finely chopped, white and green parts
$1/2$ cup chopped parsley
$1/2$ cup chopped fresh dill
$1 1/2$ cups Feta cheese, grated or crumbled
5   eggs
$1/2$ cup semolina flour
1   cup quality olive oil
$1/2$ cup milk
    Salt and pepper
10   leaves phyllo dough
$1/2$ cup sesame seeds

Preheat the oven to 350°. In a large mixing bowl, add the spinach, leeks, scallions, parsley, and dill, and toss. Add the cheese and toss again. Add the eggs and then the semolina. Work the eggs and flour into the mixture with your hands. After it is well incorporated, pour $1/2$ cup of the olive oil over all and use a wooden spoon to coat the mixture well. Add the milk and season with salt and pepper to taste. Mix all of the ingredients together again.

Brush a 9x13-inch baking pan with olive oil. Line the bottom of the pan with a leaf of phyllo. Brush with olive oil and repeat with another 4 leaves. Evenly spread the spinach mixture over the layered and oiled phyllo. Add 5 more leaves, brushing each with oil. Bake for about 45 minutes or until the phyllo is golden brown and the mixture inside is piping hot. (Add the sesame seeds, if desired, about 5 minutes before the dish is cooked.) Yield: 50 appetizer portions. ◆

Lamb Roulade of Yogurt and Feta Cheese with an Olive Sauce

Stuffed with yogurt, herbs, roasted peppers, and cheese, this lamb makes a perfect *meze* dish, cooked by Chef Stephan DeMichelis. Ask your butcher to trim and butterfly a rack of lamb and to package a pound of lamb bones for the broth. A lamb broth is made as the basis for the olive sauce.

====

3   tablespoons olive oil
1   pound lamb bones
3   tablespoons fresh basil, chopped, and a few sprigs for garnish
1   tablespoon chopped garlic
2   teaspoons fresh rosemary leaves
2   cups red wine
2   pounds boneless rack of lamb
¼   cup plain yogurt
2   red bell peppers, roasted and cut julienne (see method page 209)
4   ounces Feta cheese, crumbled
    Salt and pepper

Sauce:
8   Black Calamata olives, pits removed
    Lamb broth

====

Heat 1 tablespoon of the olive oil in a saucepan. Place the lamb bones in the pan with 1 tablespoon of the basil, garlic, and 1 teaspoon of the rosemary. Add the red wine and then enough water to cover the bones. Simmer the broth over medium heat and reduce to 1 ½ cups. Add the remaining 2 tablespoons olive oil to give a thicker consistency.

Meanwhile, prepare the lamb. Preheat the oven to 350°. Open the lamb flat and paint one side with the yogurt. Sprinkle the remaining chopped basil evenly over the top. Add half of the red pepper slices, followed by the Feta cheese. Finish with the remaining red pepper and then 1 teaspoon of the rosemary. Roll the lamb up, starting with the smaller end. Tie with kitchen string. Season all over with salt and pepper. Heat a large skillet with 1 tablespoon olive oil and brown the lamb on all sides. Place in a shallow baking pan and bake until the lamb is medium rare, about 20 to 25 minutes.

To make the olive sauce, pour the lamb juices into the saucepan containing the lamb broth. Stir and then strain the liquid into a blender. Add the olives and remaining 1 tablespoon olive oil and salt and pepper to taste. Blend until smooth.

Remove the cooked lamb from the oven and slice about ½-inch-thick slices. Drape with the olive sauce. Top with sprigs of basil for garnish. Yield: 10 slices. ◆

E N G L A N D

Westminster Abbey

A toffee pudding from a farmhouse kitchen

Sea bass with scallops at Le Manoir Aux Quat' Saisons

The Muse of the Flambé and the Temptations of the Table

Chef Raymond Blanc

LE MANOIR AUX QUAT' SAISONS, GREAT MILTON

Raymond Blanc is a chef who has made an indelible mark on those who know food in the United Kingdom. Raymond came to England from a small town in his native France, in 1972, and his restlessness for fine food drove him to help sprout a revolution for high culinary standards in Great Britain.

This quest led him on many courageous missions, such as the night he sneaked into the garden of a vegetable producer. Raymond was tired of vegetables that were overgrown for profit. He wanted to pick them at the right size and flavor. But as he did so, he was almost caught in the act of trespassing. The shadow of a tall, burly Englishman eclipsed the much smaller Frenchman. Fearing for his life, Raymond scampered out of the field.

Raymond Blanc is a culinary crusader who has taken many risks to change cooking for the better. You do not have to be a chef to feel reverence for the man who teaches that cooking is an act of giving and a very special medium through which love can flourish. In his words, "The table is a very strong symbol of togetherness, friendship, of the celebration of life, and of course, sensuality."

The chef spends nearly as much time pontificating on the virtues of his craft as he does cooking. For example, Chef Blanc inherited his talent from his ancestors, and he adds, "possibly God, whose dubious blessing it seems to have been that I should be kissed by the muse of the flambé and so enter the world of cuisine." And the tumble into that world proved to be as adventurous and intrepid as the chef himself.

> "
> *I'm here to tempt you. Like in the Garden of Eden, I stretch out my hand with food – its textures, tastes, colors – to help you express your sensuality.*
> "
>
> CHEF RAYMOND BLANC

The dovecote honeymoon suite

Characteristically, he would go out as a youngster at four o'clock in the morning to hunt wild mushrooms, search for snails, or fish for trout. However, it was not for culinary reasons, but rather the thrill of the chase and the quiet poetry and passion found on times like the one when he went foraging for wild asparagus. He searched for days and found nothing. Then one morning, as the sun came pouring through the trees, "I saw a million little heads, popping up toward the light. It was so magnificent. I knew we had hit it rich," describes the chef.

All of this interaction, gave this culinary priest a respect for nature that would someday form the basis of his cooking philosophies. Meanwhile, he pursued a career as a nurse. "I wanted to be Mother Teresa and nothing less," he recalls. But working in a children's leukemia ward, he could not face the innocent young deaths and do his best job. And since, in his own words, "Mediocrity haunts me," he left, unsure of what to do next.

Then one day, he had a revelation. "I felt I had come across that patch of wild asparagus again." An outdoor restaurant hosted tables with romantic couples and beautiful food. Raymond knew from that moment that if he were a chef, he could create the environment conducive to this "celebration of life and the receiving of food." He boldly searched out the owner and demanded that he be hired. But the owner threw him out. Next day, Raymond came back. "You must believe me. I will be a great chef someday. You must take me on," he begged.

The owner moaned that at twenty, Raymond was too old to be considering a career as chef. Most started at the age of fourteen. But the proprietor finally offered him a menial job in the kitchen. Raymond ravaged through every cookbook he could find and learned quickly. He began to tell the head chef how to improve his cooking — insisting that the chef added too much ginger and was making sauce too salty. Raymond left the restaurant one day with a broken nose from the copper skillet the angry chef had thrown at him.

When he reached British soil, Raymond found the opportunity to build a better culinary world in the United Kingdom. "I had to change the thinking of the suppliers — revolutionize the gardener before the garden," he explains. He took a job as a waiter and was later given the position of chef. In a short time, he garnered critical acclaim from all over England. All eyes were on him to find out what to do next.

By 1977, he opened his beloved Le Manoir aux Quat' Saisons, a fifteenth-century manor house, where he has created a fantasyland and the channel for food to elicit compassion and romance. "I'm here to tempt you," he says. "Like in the Garden of Eden, I stretch out my hand with food — its textures, tastes, colors — to help you express your sensuality." He advises that, "You need to do that for your own guests at home."

Raymond Blanc views cooking as an act of love: "Putting food into a microwave oven is not an act of love. We are losing our creativity. It is essential to rediscover it and at least once in awhile, take the time to cook with your hands and heart. I know it is difficult because of today's pressures, but if you think of it as giving love, you will find the time. We must get back to the table. A loving family will nourish a loving society."

Located just seven miles south of the famous university town of Oxford, Le Manoir is resplendent with mazes of pristine herb gardens and bounteous rows of vegetables. Every room is individually decorated as though an elegant guest room in someone's home. The centerpiece of the grounds is a seventeenth-century dovecote that was a love-making nest for birds before Raymond saw fit to make it a love chamber for his own guests.

In the words borrowed from the old song, "Love is all around you" at Le Manoir aux Quat'

Saisons, from the table to the guest rooms and the gardens — just as Raymond Blanc designed it to be. ◆

Editor's Note: Raymond Blanc is the author of several cookbooks, including Cooking for Friends, *which is suggested for further reading and is available from Le Manoir (See Directory page 218).*

> *You must believe me. I will be a great chef someday. You must take me on, he begged.*

Scallop-Stuffed Sea Bass with Roasted Herbs and Sauces of Fennel with Cardamom and Rosemary Butter

After de-boning a whole sea bass, you will be stuffing the fish cavity with a mixture of scallops and Swiss chard. The bass will be sliced, baked, and then served with two delicious and unusual sauces and a purée of fennel. You will need to start preparing this recipe first thing in the morning as the stuffed fish needs 6 hours to rest.

Fennel Sauce and Purée:

- 2 tablespoons chopped shallots
- 1 cup baby fennel, finely chopped, plus 4 pieces (about 1x3 inches each for the purée garnish)
- 3 tablespoons olive oil
  Zest of 1 orange
  Sprig of fresh thyme
- 1 teaspoon ground cardamom
- 2/3 cup chicken stock
  Salt and pepper
  Lemon juice

Rosemary Butter Sauce:

- 1 tablespoon white wine vinegar
- 2 tablespoons white wine
- 1 tablespoon finely chopped shallots
- 1 small twig fresh rosemary (leaves and stem), chopped
- 1/4 cup unsalted butter, cold
  Salt and pepper
- 1 tablespoon lemon juice

Roasted Herbs:

- 1 1/2 teaspoons dried fennel
- 1/2 teaspoon dried orange peel
- 1 stick of lemon grass, split
- 1/2 teaspoon dried ginger
- 4 star anis
- 1/2 cup olive oil

Tarragon Butter:

- 1 tablespoon fresh tarragon leaves, blanched
- 1 1/2 tablespoons soft butter

Stuffed Sea Bass:

- 2 pounds sea bass (1 1/2 pounds de-boned)
- 1/2 pound sea scallops
- 6 large leaves Swiss chard
  Salt and pepper
  Lemon juice, optional

To make the fennel sauce, sauté the shallots and chopped fennel in 2 tablespoons of the olive oil in a small skillet or saucepan with low sides for about 1 minute or just until translucent. Do not let brown. Add the orange zest, thyme, and cardamom. Add the chicken stock. Bring to a boil and then simmer,

Chef Blanc enjoys displaying artwork such as this romantic sculpture.

stirring constantly at low heat for 45 minutes or until slightly browned.

Meanwhile, make the fennel purée. Add the 4 pieces of fennel to a blender with 1 tablespoon of olive oil. Whirl until emulsified and pour through a cheesecloth or strainer. Enliven with salt, pepper, and lemon juice to taste. Set aside until later when it will be used as a garnish.

Prepare the rosemary butter sauce by combining the vinegar, white wine, shallots, and rosemary in a small saucepan on medium-high heat. Reduce by half. Whisk in the butter and pass through a cheesecloth or fine-mesh strainer. Add salt, pepper, and lemon juice. Set aside.

Fry all of the herbs in the olive oil until browned lightly and just crisp. Reserve the oil for later use. Combine the tarragon leaves with the butter. Set aside.

To prepare the fish, trim off the fins and tail, and remove the head. Start at the head end and bone

continued on page 180

down the backbone around the rib cage. Do this on each side of the backbone, keeping the belly intact. Remove the insides and bones, scoring (carefully with a sharp knife) the membrane that covers the thin flesh of the belly. Or, have your fishmonger do this for you.

Brush scallops and outside skin of the sea bass with the tarragon butter. Wrap scallops in Swiss chard and stuff into the belly cavity, following the shape of the fish. Starting in the middle, tie the bass with kitchen string at $1/2$-inch intervals, making sure both sides of the skin meet. Allow to rest for 6 hours in the refrigerator.

When the stuffed bass has rested, preheat the oven to 350°. Cut 2-inch slices of bass. (You will get 6 or 7 slices.) Place the roasted herbs all around the bottom of a baking sheet. Place the bass slices on top and baste during cooking with the reserved oil from the roasted herbs. Bake 15 minutes, or until the oil is absorbed.

To assemble the dish, heat the fennel and rosemary sauces and flash-heat the bass slices for 2 minutes. Heat your dinner plates and place a serving-size spoonful of fennel sauce in the center. Cut 2-inch slices of sea bass and remove the strings. Place a slice of fish on top of the sauce. Add the fennel purée and the rosemary butter sauce in vertical lines across the plates. Check seasoning. Add salt, pepper, and lemon juice, if needed. Yield: 6 servings. ◆

Wine Suggestion

The layered and richly textured flavors of **Moët & Chandon Vintage** contribute a hint of toasted brioche combined with ripe fruit to make this champagne a regal companion to the elegant sea bass and scallops preparation. It pairs well with the sensual combination of fennel, cardamom, and rosemary.

Palette Biscuit with Dabs of Sorbet

Chef Raymond Blanc makes his sorbet in Le Manoir's kitchen, but you can purchase your own, or make some of the sorbets in this cookbook (see index). This faux palette is even a nice base for colorful ice creams. Follow the directions here to make a biscuit with wood-grain effect (out of chocolate) in the shape of a palette. Then just add various sorbet flavors in the style of quenelles as though dabs of paint. The palette is really easy to make and the effect will delight your guests. Chef Blanc also prepares a pulled-sugar paintbrush, as you see in the photos. Pulled sugar garnishes are an artform, made by experienced pastry chefs. I suggest asking your baker to make the paintbrush for you, if you would like to have it on the dessert.

Equipment:

1   10x14-inch cake board (corrugated cardboard sold for cake platters in household stores)
1   8x10-inch clear mylar stencil sheet from craft store
1   X-acto knife with #11 blade
1   paper wood-grain template (provided on page 182)
1   palette template (provided on page 182)
    Scotch or masking tape

Photocopy and cut out the palette template on page 182, enlarging it by approximately 225 percent to bring it to roughly 8 inches tall by 10 inches wide. Place the paper palette template on the cake board and tape the ends and sides with scotch tape or masking tape. Cut along both of the black lines, using the X-acto knife. Then remove the template and place it and the cardboard palette aside, discarding the solid center of the cardboard palette.

Photocopy and cut out the wood-grain template on page 182, enlarging it by approximately 225 percent to bring it to just shy of 8 inches tall by 10 inches wide. Place the paper wood-grain template on mylar and tape the ends and sides with scotch tape or masking tape. Cut out the solid black lines. Set aside and proceed to make the biscuit batter.

continued on page 183

A confectionery palette hosts ice cream and a sugar-pulled paintbrush in Le Manoir's dovecote honeymoon suite. The papier mâché *doves still appear to be flitting about even as they hold a canopy of soft fabric. The striped cabana is the guest room closet.*

Enlarge templates on photo copier at 225%, enough to bring each template to an 8x10-inch size.

Wood-Grain Imitation:

- 2 tablespoons unsweetened cocoa powder
- 1 tablespoon sugar
- 1/2 cup water

Palette Biscuit:

- 1/4 cup soft butter
- 3/4 cup powdered sugar
- 1/4 cup egg whites (approximately 2 large egg whites)
- 1/4 cup all-purpose flour
- 1/8 teaspoon salt

Garnish:

- 5 different sorbet or ice cream flavors
- 4 pastry brushes made out of pulled sugar (optional)

For the wood-grain imitation: Mix the cocoa powder, sugar, and water together. Heat carefully until this mixture thickens. Whisk well. Allow to cool down.

Grease the cookie sheet, and place mylar stencil on it. Coat the stencil with chocolate mix, using a pastry brush. Once coated, remove stencil leaving chocolate wood-grain imprint on pan. Put in freezer for 30 minutes.

To make the biscuit mix: While the imprinted tray is freezing, prepare the biscuit. Soften the butter, add the powdered sugar and mix well. Add the egg whites slightly beaten, then the flour and salt, and mix until smooth.

To make the palette: Remove the imprinted tray from the freezer. Place the cardboard palette on the tray and spread biscuit mixture inside it, until level with the top of the inside edge. Remove the cardboard palette prior to baking. Repeat this process for three other palettes. (They should fit onto one baking tray.)

To bake the palette: Place the tray in the preheated oven for about 4 minutes or until the mixture is partly baked. Remove the tray from the oven and use a pastry cutter to cut out a disk from the painter's palette for the thumb hole. Replace in the oven until golden color. Remove from the oven and use a palette knife to remove the cooked painter's palette from the tray, turning it upside down. Allow to cool on a flat surface. Reserve.

To serve, quenelle five different sorbets or ice creams onto the painter's palette and serve. Yield: 4 palettes. ◆

Wine Suggestion

The exotic, rich fruit flavors found in this dessert wine make it a particularly tasteful accompaniment to a fruit sorbet or any dessert that calls for fruit. **Eiswein** (ice wine) is made from very ripe, frozen bunches of grapes that are harvested by hand during the early morning hours of winter.

The Culinary Scents of Yesterday Stirred His Career

Chef Simon Traynor

PARK LANE HOTEL, PICCADILLY

A bird-of-paradise design in silk moiré hugs the walls, and gold-leaf trim etches the moldings of Bracewell's, the premier restaurant at the Park Lane Hotel — one of London's finest places to dine. "I like it best when you walk in that room and the candles have just been lit, before the guests are to arrive. I can feel what a wonderful dining experience they are in for," says Chef Simon Traynor, of the elegant, seventy-seat Louis XVI-style room.

It is one of the little pleasures he often allows himself after a day down below in the hotel's prestigious kitchens. As head chef to Bracewell's, two other restaurants, and thirty-five staff members he describes as "a collection of knowledge and experience," Chef Traynor is a sensuous individual who takes it all out on his cuisine.

All of the senses play a role in Simon's love of cooking. It has been that way since childhood, for he still remembers how the smells and tastes of the kitchen were all he could think about. "There was the roast beef cooking on Sundays; the casserole baking in the winter-time; and the egg and bacon sizzling in the morning. They wafted past me — dream-like, mellowed me, and put me into a mood of appreciation. They stirred me. I wanted to investigate further. How were those smells created?"

> 66
>
> *The difference between what one person does with a recipe and another with the same recipe is the energy that each one puts into that dish.*
>
> 99
>
> CHEF SIMON TRAYNOR

And it is the moment of anticipation — just before the meal — that Simon savors most. "I enjoy standing there in the empty dining room, listening to the whispers of satisfaction that I know will soon fill the room." ◆

English Vegetable Double-Decker with Polenta

A tower of vegetables, potato rosti, and polenta comprise this interesting appetizer or lunch delight. It is bound to become a staple of your kitchen recipe file.

He went to culinary college to find out and then worked at some of England's top hotels and one in Hamburg. Chef Traynor has often been brought on board because of his management as well as his culinary skills. The chef says he likes to draw from his staff so that the best will emerge from the kitchen.

Chef Traynor was the rare child who actually ate everything on his plate — always. He was just too curious, too reverent, and too aware that he was sampling art to leave any behind. "I would ask myself, 'How did we get this far?'"

Chef Traynor has some ideas. It starts with today's emphasis on top quality ingredients. Next, the chef bonds with his food: "You look at food. Food looks at you. A vibration occurs between you and it. Your imagination runs away as you see the balance of flavors, textures in the raw food, and what you can do with it."

Cooking, the chef agrees, starts with the basics. But he says anything beyond that comes from the strength within yourself: "The difference between what one person does with a recipe and another with the same recipe is the energy that each one puts into that dish. Every meal you eat — even just sitting down to wine and cheese and a good loaf of bread — should be savored."

8	round polenta rings (see recipe page 206 or use fresh-purchased polenta)
4	potato rosti or potato pancakes (see recipe page 208)
1	cup vegetables (julienne of carrots, onions, and mixed green bell peppers of choice)
½	cup butter
½	cup sliced wild mushrooms of choice
¼	cup chopped fresh chives
	Salt and pepper
1	cup cooked tomato sauce
1	cup shredded Cheddar cheese

continued on page 186

The changing of the guard at Buckingham Palace

Make the polenta rings and the potato rosti. Keep warm. Blanch strips of vegetables and refresh in cold water. Set aside until needed.

Preheat the oven to 350°. In a medium skillet, melt the butter and cook the mushrooms until tender and lightly browned. Combine drained vegetables and mushrooms in a bowl and toss. Add the chives and season with salt and pepper. Set aside.

To assemble the double-deckers, begin by putting a potato pancake in the center of each of 4 serving plates. Divide half of the vegetables among the 4 plates. Then place a polenta patty on top. Top the polenta patties with the remaining vegetables and place the last ring of polenta on top.

Add the cheese overtop and place in the oven to bake for about 8 to 10 minutes or until hot and the cheese has melted. Heat the tomato sauce, and when the double-decker is ready, pour the sauce around the side of the vegetable tower. Yield: 4 servings. ◆

In the city of the double-decker bus, the chef's double-decker polenta with vegetables makes its own lofty statement.

Wine Suggestion

The medium-bodied **Aziano Chianti Classico** displays a luscious fruit character that will make it a perfect partner with the pronounced flavors of the fresh herbs, the earthy richness of the wild mushrooms, and the hearty polenta, potatoes, and cheese in Chef Traynor's vegetable dish.

Mini-Woolton Pies

The Park Lane Hotel integrates its cuisine with world events and other matters of historical significance. Chef Traynor devises special menus to suit the occasion. This recipe helped celebrate the fiftieth anniversary of D-Day. The pie was named after Lord Woolton, who conceived and promoted the dish to encourage the use of abundant supplies of locally grown vegetables. Savory pies were very popular in England because their crusts kept the contents warm so that farmers could bring them into the fields. The tradition continues today as there are bakeries all over England selling savory pies.

8 ounces short-crust pastry (see recipe page 207)
1 cup cooked, diced mixed vegetables (carrots, peas, small onions, corn)
1 cup white sauce (see recipe page 211)
¼ cup freshly chopped mixture of herbs of choice
   Salt and pepper
2 tablespoons parsley, chopped
1 cup cooked mashed potatoes

Preheat the oven to 425°. Roll out the pastry and line 4 (2-inch) flan rings. Bake the rings for 20 minutes or until golden.

Blanch the mixed vegetables and refresh in cold water. Drain well. Mix the vegetables with the white sauce. Add the herbs and season with salt and pepper to taste. Mix well.

Combine the chopped parsley with the mashed potatoes. Place the mixture evenly into the flan rings. Using a pastry bag, pipe the prepared potatoes on top of the flans. Place in the oven and heat through until potatoes have a pale golden hue (about 20 minutes). Serve with a salad. Yield: 4 servings. ◆

Wine Suggestion

The delicate floral bouquet and flavors of this Rheingau wine come naturally from the perfect ripeness of the Riesling grape of Johannisberg. The **Sichel Bereich Johannisberg** is a real treat with this vegetable dish because it contrasts so well with the quiet flavors and textures of the pie.

A war-time meal of Woolton Pie stands sentinel outside Buckingham Palace during the changing of the guard. It's Chef Traynor's salute to British cuisine.

Cooking Italian Near the Queen's Doorstep

Chef Giuseppe Sestito

HYDE PARK HOTEL, KNIGHTSBRIDGE

*S*it for ten minutes in the Park Room Restaurant at Hyde Park Hotel in London, and at least a half-dozen different images may flash by — from riders on horseback trotting along the dusty bridle paths to courtly royal carriages wheeling past. Activities at the famous Hyde Park bring a variety of wonder, curiosity, and chuckles to the tabletop. Joggers, bikers, uniformed gentlemen in royal regalia, and boys and girls from Hill House school — clad in corduroy knickerbockers — offer a touch of whimsy and patriotism. The views from the restaurant take you directly past majestic, age-old trees into historic Hyde Park.

Although born in southern Italy, Chef Giuseppe Sestito has made the Park Room restaurant — only minutes from Buckingham Palace — the setting for his much-heralded northern Mediterranean cuisine. His style is free of butters and creams. Olive oil reigns supreme. The chef orders Italian herbs and fresh cheeses, such as Bufala Mozzarella — direct from Italy.

At age twelve, Chef Sestito was cooking his own recipe for spaghetti bolognese. And after many rounds of applause, he stepped into his lifetime role. By seventeen, he took a job as apprentice chef and then traveled extensively throughout Italy, Switzerland, and the United States, enhancing his skills at top kitchens.

"I remember tasting the foods my family

cooked. I fell in love with food at an early age and have never let it go," says the chef. "I love bringing all of the fresh ingredients together and making people happy."

The curious stuffed artichokes you see on page 190 are just one of the chef's original creations, employing his philosophy that cooking should be simple and easy. His main line of advice is: "Always taste your food at every stage, as honest flavor cannot be added at the last minute."

Diners at the Hyde Park Hotel can watch the royal horse guard parade right by the restaurant windows.

66

Always taste your food at every stage, as honest flavor cannot be added at the last minute.

99

CHEF GIUSEPPE SESTITO

While it may seem odd featuring Italian food in the heart of Great Britain, the Hyde Park is an international hotel — also hosting the talents of Michelin-star Chef Marco Pierre White, who cooks classic French. Guests of the hotel have their choice. But across the street nothing changes. The sun sets and street lamps twinkle. The park slows down. But the excitement still parades by as romance unfolds again on the tabletops thanks to restaurant menu choices such as Chef Sestito's Ravioli with Black Truffles and his Tuscany Farro Soup with Cannelini Beans. ◆

Stuffed Artichokes with Ricotta Cheese and Basil Coulis

Buy the largest artichokes you can find for this wonderful appetizer, which will give you added reason to consider the artichoke when entertaining. This recipe combines chopped artichoke hearts with Ricotta and basil, stuffed into an artichoke shell.

8	large artichokes, washed
½	cup Parmesan cheese
1	cup extra virgin olive oil
2	tablespoons chopped fresh garlic
2	cups quality white wine
	Water
2	medium bunches fresh basil
1 ¾	cups Ricotta cheese
1	small bunch fresh mint
	Salt to taste
	Juice of 1 small lemon

continued on page 190

One of Hyde Park's familiar striped lounge chairs sets the scene for Artichoke Hearts with Ricotta Cheese and Basil Coulis beside Serpentine Lake. The hotel's doorman lent us his hat and gloves, worn ever so symbolically back at the hotel.

Place the cleaned artichokes in a 6-quart saucepan with 2 tablespoons of the olive oil, garlic, white wine, and salt to taste. Cook over high heat, bringing the mixture to a boil. Cook until all of the liquid evaporates. Add cold water to the pot, just enough to cover the artichokes. Simmer for 1 $\frac{1}{2}$ hours. Remove from the heat. Drain and let cool.

When the artichokes have cooled enough to handle, remove the center part of the artichoke or the large heart and chop.

Chop 1 bunch of the basil and mint finely and mix with the Ricotta cheese, chopped hearts, and $\frac{1}{2}$ cup of the olive oil. Fill the artichokes with the Ricotta cheese mixture. Sprinkle the Parmesan cheese overtop. Place the artichokes under the broiler to melt and brown the cheese.

Chop the remaining basil and prepare a dressing with olive oil and the lemon juice. Place a warm artichoke on a serving plate and spoon the dressing overtop. Yield: 4 servings. ◆

Tiramisu

There are many versions of this wonderful Italian dessert from Venice — some more elegant than others. This rendition is just right and will do what the title of the recipe means. It will indeed pick you up. Mascarpone cheese is a double-whipped cream cheese available in gourmet stores and supermarkets.

---

1 pound premade sponge (angel food) cake
    (see recipe on page 212 or purchase cake)
1 cup espresso coffee
3 eggs, separated
1 cup sugar
¼ cup heavy cream
¾ pound Mascarpone cheese
3 tablespoons unsweetened cocoa powder

Soak the spongecake in the espresso. Set aside.

In a large mixing bowl, whisk together the yolks and sugar and then whisk in the heavy cream and then the Mascarpone cheese. In a separate, smaller bowl, whisk the egg whites until light and fluffy. Slowly add this to the Mascarpone cheese and whisk the mixture until soft peaks form.

Lightly grease a 9x9-inch glass baking dish. Place half the cake in the dish and spread half of the cheese mixture overtop. Place the remaining cake on top of the cheese and spread the remaining cheese mixture over all. Chill in the refrigerator for 2 hours. Just before serving, remove from the refrigerator and dust cocoa powder overtop with a fine sieve. Serve. Yield: 8 to 10 servings. ◆

Spirit Suggestion

COGNAC
Hennessy
X.O
ALC 40% BY VOL (80 PROOF) Hennessy Cognac France   750 ML

The X.O designation used throughout the Cognac region was created by Maurice Hennessy in the nineteenth century. Originally, this blend of old cognac was reserved for the Hennessy family and friends. Some of the fine old cognacs in this blend are seventy years old, making **Hennessy X.O** rich, full-bodied, and unctuous. This cognac goes well with the equally respected and traditional Tiramisu.

The international flavor of London is evident in this Italian dessert of Tiramisu below Tower Bridge.

Watching the Cows Milk and the Apples Press: A Day in the Life of a Country Chef

Chef Caron Cooper

FOSSE FARMHOUSE, WILTSHIRE

*T*he world's great chefs no longer work only in famous cities. At establishments tucked into the countryside on back roads, some of the most memorable cooking and eating takes place every day. And so it is at Caron Cooper's 1750 Fosse Farmhouse in Nettleton Shrub, a small village where the historic Fosse Way was the only passage cut by the ancient Romans to travel through this part of England.

Here, the chef, who has received national and international fame for her simple style, is surrounded by miles of fruitful land that yields the basis for the food she cooks. From a small mustard producer, a crayfish farmer, and an apple-brandy/cider maker to a clotted-cream dairy and acres of pick-your-own strawberries and asparagus, Caron Cooper's market is only a farm away.

"Food is fun and shopping is the beginning of that experience," she says. "Going to a supermarket is not interesting. At a fresh market, the producers are delighted to explain where their goods come from, how they are grown, and the joy that it gives them to grow them for you."

Caron purposely chose such an environment, because she believes cooking is an exercise in creating flavors based on what is "locally best, beautifully produced, and tastes good." When you have those ingredients, she theorizes, "you don't have to be a brilliant cook to create beautiful flavors." She advises that "Home cooks should be happy with what they are doing. Relax, enjoy, and don't agonize over complicated recipes. Be confident. Go for it."

Caron's cooking philosophies were shaped from the heart at kitchens in southwest France where she bought a cottage. She was invited into her neighbors' kitchens and the natives taught her market shopping: how to select produce, talk to the producers and appreciate their work.

The rest of her cooking background stemmed from, as she puts it, "five years of sneaking around professional kitchens," while she followed her first career as an international (traveling) disc jockey. Constantly staying at hotels, she "got so bored" that she found her way to the kitchens to talk with the chefs.

Caron's cooking methods produce country cuisine in her small dining room at the five-room farmhouse and tea shop. One day, her cooking and lifestyle caught the interest of a Japanese tourist who opened the door for Caron to showcase her farm cooking internationally. Today, she spends time in Japan, representing English farmhouse cuisine, leading seminars, and giving cooking demonstrations.

At the farmhouse, her work revolves around the kitchen. And with the help of her mother, June, she is able to keep the tea shop, bed-and-breakfast, and her 12-seat dining room all going. The chef has boundless energy, having restored five historic houses before Fosse Farm. She reasons, simply: "Tomorrow is another day." But for her guests, the tiny blackboard she puts out each morning — announcing the evening menu — reminds them that it is tonight they are looking forward to at Fosse Farmhouse. ◆

> *You don't have to be a brilliant cook to create beautiful flavors. Home cooks should be happy . . . relax, enjoy and don't agonize over complicated recipes. Go for it.*
>
> CHEF CARON COOPER

Wiltshire is home to the quaint villages and winding lanes of the southern Cotswolds.

A small blaze warms the dining room at Fosse Farmhouse. Roast Pork with Apple, Mustard, a Honey Cream Sauce, and Baked Apples is about to be served.

Roast Pork with Apple, Mustard, a Honey Cream Sauce, and Baked Apples

Marinade:
- 1 tablespoon honey (the thinner the better)
- 2 tablespoons coarse-grain mustard
- 2 tablespoons apple brandy

Pork:
- 3 ½ pounds loin of pork
- 2 tablespoons unsalted butter
- Coarse salt

Baked Apples:
- 6 large Pippin apples, cored but not peeled
- Cinnamon and sugar mixture to taste

Sauce:
- ½ cup hard cider or non-alcoholic cider
- ½ cup chicken stock
- Reserved marinade
- 2 tablespoons crème fraîche (see page 213) or heavy cream

In a small bowl, mix together the honey, mustard, and apple brandy. Brush over the loin of pork and leave covered in the refrigerator for 24 hours. After marinating, pour off the marinade and reserve for the sauce.

Preheat the oven to 350°. Pat the loin of pork dry. Then score all over with a knife. Rub butter onto the loin and sprinkle with the coarse salt. Place the loin on a rack pan to catch juices and roast for 2 hours.

Meanwhile, season the apples to taste with sugar and cinnamon. Make a shallow cut through the skin all around the apple, about ¹/₃ of the way down. Place the apples into a round cake tin or dish and baste with some of the fat from the pork. Cook on a lower shelf in the oven for the last 30 to 45 minutes of the cooking time for the pork.

Remove the pork from the oven when cooked. Keep warm. Stir the cider into the meat juices on the stovetop. Boil for 2 minutes. Stir in the chicken stock with the reserved marinade and boil for 3 more minutes, stirring frequently, scraping up the pan drippings. Add the crème fraîche and stir over the heat for 2 more minutes. Strain into a sauce boat or server.

Arrange the apples around the pork and serve accompanied by the sauce. Yield: 6 servings. ◆

Wine Suggestion

The **Goldtröpfchen** (little drops of gold) vineyard of the Mosel region produces some of Germany's most delicate and complex wines. The Riesling grape yields ripe fruit flavors and a distinctive crispness, pairing well with the roast pork. The Riesling, prized as one of the world's finest varieties, is so flavorful that it will stand up to ingredients like apple, mustard, and honey, found in Chef Cooper's tasteful and textured farmhouse dish.

Caron Cooper's version of sticky toffee pudding is on display here in her country kitchen with the inn's guestbook and items from Caron's extensive collection of kitchen memorabilia.

Sticky Toffee Pudding with Vanilla Sauce

"They sheepishly ask for seconds when I serve this for dessert," says chef and innkeeper Caron Cooper. Your guests will probably do the same with this version of the famous pudding (a cake-like dessert) by Caron. The pudding freezes well with the sauce on top. Reheat in the microwave or conventional oven to serve.

Pudding:

- 1   cup water
- 1   cup chopped dates
- 1   teaspoon baking soda
- 1/4   cup butter
- 1   cup sugar
- 2   eggs
- 1   cup all-purpose flour
- 1/2   teaspoon vanilla extract

Sauce:

- 3/4   cup granulated dark brown sugar
- 1/2   cup heavy cream
- 1/2   teaspoon vanilla extract
- 1/2   cup butter

Preheat the oven to 325°. Bring the water and dates to a boil in a small saucepan. As soon as they boil, remove from the heat and stir in the baking soda. Leave to cool slightly.

In a large mixing bowl, cream together the butter and sugar. Gradually add in the eggs. Fold in the flour and stir in the dates with their liquid. Stir in the vanilla and butter. Pour into an 8x11-inch baking pan and bake 45 minutes or until browned and firm. Remove from the heat and let cool down some.

To make the sauce, place all of the sauce ingredients into a small saucepan. Mix and bring to the boil, stirring continuously. Simmer for 3 minutes. When the pudding is just warm, spread with a thick coating of the sauce and cool to room temperature. Serve. Yield: 10 to 12 servings. ◆

Spirit Suggestion

A glass of this rich **Hennessy V.S Cognac** — with dominating notes of oak followed by light aromas of hazelnut — perfectly complements the flavor in this classic English pudding.

Steeping in Relaxation
The Charms of Afternoon Tea

It is true. The British know how to do it best when it comes to ceremony. But when afternoon tea time rolls around, do not be fooled. The absence of white gloves, fancy linens, and bone china in no way diminishes the spirit of a comforting *cuppa* and fresh-baked scones with finger sandwiches. Drinking a cup of tea in the afternoon is the great equalizer in England and anywhere, for it does not mean a stuffy ceremony need take place. No matter what "muddle of a head" you have, troubles vanish once the tea leaves' flavor hits the taste buds.

England is rampant with places to enjoy afternoon tea — from the luxurious hotels in London to the quiet tea shops in Bath and the nearby Cotswolds. The style of presentation varies along with what is served and the environment. Only the method of tea preparation is a constant.

In the big city, Brown's Hotel treats you to a sumptuous respite in an English country-style library, just off the lobby. In Bath, the Pump House entices you with its classical music and silver butlers. And at Fosse Farmhouse in Nettleton Shrub, the gardens, antiques, and general sense of whimsy invite you to enjoy the clotted cream and strawberries beneath the beams and remnants of feeding posts in a reformed horse stable that is now the teahouse.

While they do not share the daily English penchant for taking tea, a dream of many Americans is nonetheless to ride down a country lane and stop along the way at a small tea shop for a cup and a sweet. Visitors do just that when they see the sign out for the Fosse Farmhouse tea shop, and similar tea haunts that dot the English countryside.

World Class Cuisine filmed the process of making afternoon tea in the sitting room of the Hyde Park Hotel. The Hyde Park's recipe for serving the revered brew is on page 200. ◆

Tea is served all afternoon in the Fosse Farmhouse tea room. Brits motoring by, stop in as do tourists in search of a hot cuppa and a buttery scone or two. The tea room is almost always open in true English tradition.

Making the Proper Cup of Tea

Draw water for the tea kettle from a cold tap. Heat the water on the stove over high heat to just boiling.

Choose tea leaves of top quality.

Warm the ceramic, pottery or porcelain teapot by filling it with hot water. Empty the pot of the water.

Fill the tea ball or infuser loosely, allowing 1 teaspoon for each cup of water and 1 extra teaspoon for the pot, or place the loose tea directly into the pot. Add the tea ball or infuser to the pot.

Pour the boiling water into the teapot. Allow the tea to steep for about five minutes. Pour a little milk into the cup.

Pour the tea into cups, using a hand-held strainer to catch any stray tea leaves.

Always keep a teapot of hot water nearby to dilute the tea, which often has the habit of growing strong and tepid when sitting idly. ◆

Fosse Farmhouse Fruit and Bread Pudding

Perfect with tea any time of year, you may substitute for fresh fruit in season. This recipe requires a 24-hour advance preparation time as it must mold in the refrigerator.

4 small red plums, pitted and chopped
1 pound ripe red strawberries
1/2 pound fresh blueberries
1/2 pound raspberries
1/2 pound red Bing cherries, pitted and cut in half
2 tablespoons sugar
1 1/2 tablespoons cassis
1/4 cup white wine
2 teaspoons kirsch
6 slices day-old bread

Simmer the fruits in a medium saucepan with the sugar, cassis, white wine, and kirsch for about 5 minutes or until the fruit is soft.

Line a 6-inch glass mixing bowl entirely with five slices of the bread, leaving no gaps. Strain the fruit from the juice in the pan and spoon the fruit into the bowl. Pour in half of the cooked liquid and reserve the rest for later use. Use the last slice of bread to form a lid on top of the fruit.

Place a saucer on top of the pudding, just inside the rim of the bowl, and put a heavy weight on top of the saucer. Refrigerate for 24 hours.

Gently release the pudding from the bowl, employing a sharp knife to loosen edges. Invert the bowl and tap out the pudding onto a serving plate. Serve with reserved fruit juice and freshly whipped cream or ice cream. Yield: 4 to 6 servings. ◆

Walnut Cake with Rum Sauce

A steaming hot cup of Darjeeling, Orange Pekoe or another non-herbal tea will perfectly complement this flavorful, sweet cake from Chef Stephan DeMichelis.

===

Sauce:

3	cups water
3/4	cup sugar
1	tablespoon corn syrup or glucose sugar
2	tablespoons dark rum

Cake:

8	eggs
2	tablespoons sugar
	Zest of 1 medium lemon
2	cups (1 pound) cake flour
1 1/2	cups sugar
1	teaspoon cinnamon
1	cup coarsely chopped walnuts
8	walnut halves for garnish

===

Make the sauce first. Add the water and sugar to a saucepan and mix. Stir in the corn syrup and place over medium heat. Let simmer while preparing the cake.

Preheat the oven to 350°. Prepare the cake batter. Separate the eggs. In a small bowl, whisk the 2 tablespoons of sugar with the egg yolks and stir in the lemon zest. Set aside. In another small bowl, beat the egg whites until stiff peaks form.

In a large mixing bowl, mix together the flour, the 1 1/2 cups sugar, cinnamon, and walnuts. Fold the beaten egg yolks into the egg-white mixture with a spatula. Add to the dry ingredients, folding the eggs carefully.

Grease an 8-inch round baking pan. Pour the batter into the pan. Bake the cake for 30 to 40 minutes or until the top is golden brown and a tester inserted in the center comes clean. When the cake is ready, turn it upside down and gently release from the baking pan. Then, turn right-side up onto a serving plate.

Return to the sauce, stirring in the rum and heating through. Saturate the cake with the syrup by ladling the syrup overtop. Decorate with walnut halves around the perimeter of the cake. Yield: 8 servings. ◆

PANTRY

Irish brown bread at Marlfield House (recipe on page 206)

Goat cheese at Inagh Farm

The grass is always greener on the other side . . .

A Farm Where the 'Kids' Supply the Milk

Goat Cheese: A Special Item for Every Pantry

The clouds hovered across the Irish sky on the morning that the *World Class Cuisine* crew followed Chef John Sheedy to the farm where he buys goat cheese for recipes such as the one on page 39. Tucked deep into the countryside in an area called Inagh, about an hour south of the chef's kitchen at Ashford Castle, one of the world's smallest but most heralded goat cheese farms provides the stuff storybooks are made of.

The farm is owned by Meg and Derrick Gordon and a playful bunch of *kids* — and goats, who generously supply the milk for cheeses that are sold all over the United Kingdom. The milk comes down in buckets in the barn, much like the rain was doing as the heavens opened up on our cameras that day — in true Irish form. No matter to the goats, there was more time for frolicking all over Meg in their pen; and no matter to our crew members, who were grinning through the raindrops and mud as they taped Meg and her affectionate *children.*

Such is life on the goat cheese farm that the supposedly-retired Gordons have operated since 1980 in County Clare. The farm produces some three-and-a-half tons of cheese, using processing methods Meg learned while studying on a French farm.

"I wanted to do something that could give good health to people," Meg recalls of her first encounter with the notion of making the cheese. "I love handling the cheese. I love the feel of it," she adds as the goats rally for her attention. Onlookers hear Meg playfully coo back as she looks at her *kids,* "You're such good people. Ah, you're trying to eat my ear. Whoops, someone's eating my hair."

Goat cheese — considered a staple in French cooking for centuries and until recent times better known as *chèvre* — is becoming a popular ingredient in the cuisine of world class chefs and even home cooks. This tangy cheese is most often found in its soft form. Lower in fat and cholesterol than many cow's milk cheeses, goat cheese is a healthy alternative for nutrition-conscious consumers. In Inagh, the goats feed on the land, which Meg has enriched with herbs and maintained free of pesticides or fertilizers.

The production of goat cheese — made French-style at the Gordon farm, begins each morning after the milking. Raw milk — still in buckets — is brought inside where a starter with enzymes is added. It is then left to sit for twenty-four hours. Meg takes the temperature of the resulting cheese and tests it for acidity. If the conditions meet her approval, she strains the still-clumpy cheese through a cheesecloth and into cylindrical molds. The molds are stored in a *hot room* for another day for the cheese to become firm. The next step involves transferring the molds to the refrigerator for two to three

Meg Gordon with her kids

days. For the final step, Meg unmolds the cheese and leaves the firm rounds in the refrigerator to age for about two weeks before they are ready.

The Gordons have garnered several awards for their cheese in the goat-cheese category, and for the overall best cheese of any kind made in Ireland and the United Kingdom.

Goat cheese is now readily available in gourmet stores, health food markets, and supermarkets. Besides goat cheese recipes listed in the index, following are several other ways I like to serve the soft variety. ◆

- Make a crostini with crusty bread by spreading goat cheese overtop each piece and adding herbs and sun-dried tomatoes. Drizzle with olive oil and bake at 350° until the cheese is hot.

- Spread cheese on thin slivers of salmon and roll up.

- Core a tomato and fill it with a mixture of goat cheese, pesto, olive oil, and fresh basil.

- Spread cheese over baguette slices and coat with dried lavender and roasted almonds. Bake in a moderate oven on a cookie sheet until hot.

- Use egg-roll wrappers and stuff with goat cheese. Fold up like a won ton and fry in oil. Serve with yogurt or sour cream or plain.

- Add goat cheese to scrambled eggs with fresh herbs for a lively breakfast.

- Crumble goat cheese over garden salads.

- Grill the cheese on the barbecue and dress it up with salad leaves.

- Toss goat cheese with steamed vegetables, lemon juice, ground black pepper, and dill. ◆

Goat cheese is ladled into the mold at the Gordon farm.

Marlfield House's Irish Brown Bread

"If I was asked what is the definitive taste of Ireland, I would not hesitate to say brown bread. Quite ubiquitous, it is found in restaurants, hotels, country houses, cottages – in fact any dwelling throughout the island. Most of it is homemade, in varying weights and textures, and its flavor is complemented by creamy Irish butter, which has no peers."

This is what author Mike Bunn had to say in his book, *Ireland: The Taste and Country.* To that I add that the brown bread at Marlfield House (see photo on page 202) is among the best from any of those "restaurants, hotels, country houses…" It is perfect with any meal, including the Irish Breakfast.

2 *pounds (4 cups) brown, whole-wheat flour*
2 *teaspoons baking soda*
3 *tablespoons dark brown sugar*
4 *eggs, beaten*
4 1/3 *cups buttermilk*

Preheat the oven to 350°. In a large mixing bowl, mix together the flour, baking soda, and sugar with a wooden spoon. Add the eggs and the buttermilk and mix with the spoon, just until all of the dry ingredients are moistened and the batter is of dripping consistency. Place in 2 lightly greased 9 5/8 x 5 1/2 x 2 3/4-inch bread loaf pans and bake for 1 hour. Remove from the tins and bake for 1/2 hour longer or until the bread has a hollow sound when you tap it. Allow the bread to rest before slicing. Yield: 2 loaves. ◆

Polenta

Polenta is the Italian form of cornmeal mush. Most often fried, it is great as a side dish or — with vegetables in between layers — as a sandwich or entree such as Chef Traynor's double-decker on page 185. You may buy polenta mix in a package at a supermarket, or use this recipe.

3 1/2 *cups water*
4 *tablespoons butter*
1 *teaspoon salt*
1 *cup stone-ground, yellow cornmeal*
   Butter for frying

In a heavy saucepan over high heat, bring the water and salt to a boil. Reduce the heat to medium and add the cornmeal in a stream, whisking constantly. Cook over medium heat, stirring for 15 minutes or until thick. Stir in the butter and salt and pour batter into a greased, 9-inch, shallow baking pan. Cover and chill for 30 minutes. Invert onto a board and cut into 8 squares or rounds. Fry lightly on both sides in butter. Drain on paper towels. Keep warm. Yield: 8 patties. ◆

Quick Puff Pastry

Unlike traditional puff pastry, this recipe is less labor intensive. It may be used for both savory and sweet pastry cases. The secret to good puff pastry is not to let the butter get too cold or hot because uneven distribution can cause excessive fat run-off during baking. Be sure to read the directions thoroughly before beginning.

12	ounces unsalted butter (very cold)
1½	cups all-purpose flour
½	cup cake flour
1	teaspoon salt
½	cup ice water

Preheat the oven to 400°. Dice the butter into 1-inch squares and place into an electric mixing bowl with the flours and salt. (Make sure that the butter did not get warm while dicing, if so refrigerate until cold.) Mix the dough on low speed with the paddle attachment, until the butter is broken into ½-inch pieces (the size of chickpeas). Mix in just enough of the water to hold the dough together without making the butter pieces any smaller.

Lightly flour a flat work surface. Quickly roll the dough out to a 12-inch rectangle, making sure the dough is still cold. At this point the dough will not have come together yet and will look unevenly mixed. Fold ⅓ of the rectangle over the center, and fold the remaining ⅓ on top of the first fold. Lightly flour the top of the dough and turn it 90 degrees so that the length becomes the width. (The dough must be turned like this before each roll so that the gluten is pulled evenly to prevent deformities when baked.) Lift up the dough and lightly sprinkle flour underneath, taking up any dough that may be stuck to the work surface.

Flour the top of the dough and roll it into a rectangle a second time, making sure the surface of the dough is smooth and even. Do not handle the dough excessively or press down on the dough when rolling out; the heat from your hands can melt the butter. Remove any excess flour from the surface of the dough and fold the 2 ends to the center. Make sure the corners are even and have square edges.

Fold the dough in half like a closed book to complete the procedure. Refrigerate about 15 minutes to chill the butter and relax the gluten. Repeat the folding process twice more, remembering to chill the dough if necessary. When ready to use, remove from the refrigerator and roll out to a 12-inch rectangle ¹⁄₁₆ inch thick. Cut into desired shapes. Yield: 3 pounds. ◆

Short-Crust Pastry

Use this dough for a variety of savory crust-making needs, such as the Woolton Pies on page 186. Add to the quantity of each ingredient for recipes with larger servings.

1½	cups all-purpose flour
1	egg
½	cup butter, very cold

Sift flour in a mound on a cool, clean work surface. Make a well in the center of the mound with the back of a tablespoon. Break the egg into the well. Cut chilled butter into small pieces and place on top of flour around the edge of the well. Cut through the ingredients with a metal spatula until the mixture resembles coarse crumbs. Gather together and knead pastry with cool hands. Shape into a ball, cover with plastic wrap, and refrigerate for 30 minutes until ready to use.

For the Woolton Pies, divide pastry in four. Roll out each piece to ¼ inch. Place in flan rings; trim off edges; prick lightly all over with a fork. Bake in 425° oven for 20 minutes or until golden brown. Allow to cool and then fill accordingly. Yield: Enough for up to a 9-inch tart. ◆

Pasta Dough

For Salmon Tortellini with Pan-Fried Scallops in a Chive Butter Sauce and Fried Leeks

This wonderful pasta dish is in the Pantry section, because I wanted to give you a recipe for pasta dough. And then I said, well, why not include a use for that dough and let it be Chef Kevin Arundel's tortellini dish, pictured on page 70. You can use the dough for a variety of pastas. A pasta machine (to get the dough fine enough) is highly recommended by our recipe tester. You will be shaping the tortellini by hand, and it is surprisingly easy to do.

Pasta Dough:

- 1 cup all-purpose flour
- 2 whole eggs
- 1 egg yolk
- 1 tablespoon olive oil
   Salt

Salmon Stuffing:

- 3 ounces salmon
- 1 tablespoon egg white
- 1/4 cup heavy cream
   Cayenne pepper
- 10 sea scallops, finely diced (plus 10 more for pan-frying)

Sauce:

- 1 shallot, minced
- 1/4 cup white wine
- 1/4 cup white wine vinegar
- 1 tablespoon heavy cream
- 1/2 cup butter
   Small bunch chives, finely chopped

Garnish:

- 1/2 of a large leek, cut finely with a Mandoline or grated with a hand grater
- 4 cups cooking oil, or less for deep-frying

In a large mixing bowl, blend together the flour, eggs, and egg yolk with the olive oil and a sprinkling of salt. Shape the dough into a ball and let rest for 1 to 2 hours in the refrigerator. When the dough has rested, roll it out as thinly as possible, using the pasta maker. (From here, cut according to desired shape, if not making the tortellini.) Cut into 2-inch squares, totaling about 20 pieces. Fold over into a half-moon shape and fold to press together and fasten.

Meanwhile, prepare the tortellini stuffing. Whirl the salmon in a blender or food processor for 1 minute. Then add a sprinkling of salt and the egg white. Fold in the cream, finishing with a dash of cayenne. Fold the diced scallops into the mixture. Set aside.

Place a dollop or about 1 tablespoon of the salmon mixture onto a pasta square. Set aside and prepare the sauce. Finely chop the shallot and add to a small saucepan. Add the wine and vinegar and reduce until it reaches a syrupy consistency. Add the cream. Then whisk in the diced butter and finally the chives.

Poach the tortellini in hot water for 3 to 4 minutes. Meanwhile, pan-fry the remaining 10 scallops in butter for about 1 minute per side.

Prepare the garnish by deep-frying the leeks in hot oil until crisp. Season with salt.

To assemble the dish, coat the bottom of a serving plate with some of the sauce. Arrange the tortellini around the plate, alternately with scallops. Add the leeks in the center. Yield: 4 servings (20 tortellini). ◆

Potato Rosti

In Europe there are several names for this simple combination of shredded potatoes, fried into a potato patty with cooking oil. You will also hear it called a galette or a potato pancake, for example. Several dishes in this book call for this potato delight and instructions are included with the main recipes. Or you may use this recipe, specially prepared by Chef Simon Traynor for his English Vegetable Double-Decker with Polenta on page 185.

- 2 medium potatoes, peeled
   Salt and pepper
   Butter for frying

Shred potatoes on the large-hole side of a hand-grater or use a Mandoline, if you have one. Place the potatoes in a cheesecloth or tea towel and squeeze them of any juice. Shape them into 4-inch rounds and place them in a skillet in enough butter to coat the pan. Cook until crisp on each side. Drain on a paper towel and keep warm until ready to use. Yield: 4 to 6 patties. ◆

Moyglare Manor's Mushroom Soup

Chef Jim Cullinane's mushroom soup is a marvelous recipe to enjoy along with a salad and some crusty bread. But it is also here in the Pantry section, because it is a great base for meat, fish, or chicken casseroles.

4   tablespoons butter
8   ounces wild or button mushrooms, finely chopped
1/2   cup finely chopped onions
1   teaspoon each chopped fresh parsley and chives
4   cups chicken stock
3   tablespoons all-purpose flour
    Salt and pepper
1/2   cup heavy cream or up to 3/4 cup, if desired

In a large saucepan, melt the butter and add the mushrooms, onions, parsley, and chives. Cook over moderate heat until the onion turns translucent. Mix in the flour and cook over a gentle flame. Do not brown. Gradually add in the stock and simmer uncovered for 30 to 40 minutes. Add the mixture to a blender or food processor, just enough to liquidize. Turn back to the boil and season with salt and pepper. When heated through, stir in the cream, if desired. Yield: 4 soup servings or 1 quart for use in a recipe. ◆

Roasted Red Peppers

Roasted bell peppers are excellent in salads, sandwiches, pizza, pasta, grilled meats, or alone as a condiment on an appetizer tray. You can serve them with a variety of recipes in this book. In fact, Chef Stephan DeMichelis' yogurt-and-bell-pepper-stuffed lamb roulade on page 173, requires roasted peppers. There are just as many ways to serve the peppers, as there are to prepare them.

Chef DeMichelis simply roasts his over the flames. You may skewer a whole pepper and place it over a grill or under a broiler until the skin blackens and chars. You may remove the skin then, or seal the pepper tightly in a brown paper bag for 10 minutes. This moisturizes the pepper and makes removing the skin easier.

Use a knife to peel away the skin. Scrape away the seeds and remove the stem. Cut the pepper into 1/2-inch strips. To store up to a month, cover and refrigerate with olive oil in a jar. ◆

Tomato Concassée

This is a basic recipe for chopping and blanching tomato pulp.

2   medium tomatoes (about 1 pound)

Bring a medium saucepan of water to a boil. Stem the tomatoes and score the bottom with an X. Parboil the tomatoes in the water for 20 to 30 seconds or just until the scored edges of the skin begin to peel back. Transfer the tomatoes to a cold water bath to stop the cooking. Once they are cool enough to handle, cut the tomatoes in half horizontally, squeeze out the seeds, peel off the skin, and chop into a small dice. Yield: 1 1/2 cups. ◆

Fish Stock

2 - 3 pounds fish bones or frames
2 - 3 quarts water
    Salt

(If using whole fish frames, gut them, remove the gills, and wash them as well as the fish bones under cold running water. Cut them to fit in the stockpot.)

Put the fish bones in a large, nonreactive stockpot. Add water to cover, about 2 to 3 quarts, and salt to taste. Bring to a boil and skim the scum as it rises. Reduce the heat, cover the pot, and simmer for about 20 minutes.

Strain the stock through a colander, removing the bones. Cool, cover, and refrigerate or freeze until ready to use. Yield: 1 $\frac{1}{2}$ quarts. ◆

Beef Stock

Beef stock may be made several different ways. I love this flavorful version by Chef Stewart Cameron from Turnberry. Actually intended for his beef recipe on page 121, this may be used for any number of recipes. The addition of the tomato paste and the herbs really sets this one apart.

  2 pounds beef bones
    Salt and pepper
$\frac{1}{4}$ cup chopped onion
  2 tablespoons chopped carrot
  2 tablespoons chopped leek
  2 tablespoons chopped celery
  2 tablespoons tomato paste
  1 bay leaf
$\frac{3}{4}$ cup red wine
  1 tablespoon dried thyme
  4 cups cold water

In a medium stockpot, brown the beef bones. Add the vegetables and sweat them until they turn a golden brown. Remove any excess fat or oil. Add the tomato paste and cook for 5 minutes more. Add the wine and then the bay leaf and thyme. Add the water and bring back to a boil. Skim the surface and then turn down the heat to a simmer. Simmer gently for 2 hours then pass through a sieve. Yield: About 4 cups. ◆

Chicken Stock

  2 pounds raw or cooked chicken meat and/or bones
  2 quarts water
  2 stalks celery, cut into 1-inch pieces
  1 carrot, cut into 1-inch pieces
  1 onion, cut in half
  1 bay leaf
2 - 3 parsley stems
  6 peppercorns
    Salt

Put the chicken in the stockpot. Add the water, celery, carrot, onion, bay leaf, parsley, peppercorns, and salt to taste. (When salting the chicken stock, some of the liquid will evaporate and the stock will become more concentrated. Be careful not to oversalt). Bring to a boil and skim the scum as it rises. Reduce the heat and partially cover and simmer the stock for 1 $\frac{1}{2}$ to 2 hours. Add more water if the liquid evaporates and the bones or vegetables are not covered.

Strain the stock through a colander into a large bowl and cool it uncovered. Refrigerate the stock and remove the congealed fat from the surface. Store the stock in the refrigerator for several days or freeze it in smaller containers. Yield: 1 $\frac{1}{2}$ quarts. ◆

Vegetable Stock
(Nick Nairn's Nage)

So many recipes ask for either beef, chicken or fish stock. Here is a refreshing alternative. Chef Nick Nairn, from Braeval Old Mill in Scotland, incorporated this recipe in his dish on page 131, but it is presented here as a base stock to be used in a multitude of recipes that would normally require a meat stock.

1   medium onion, diced
1   leek, white part only
1   rib celery, diced
4   large carrots, diced
1   head garlic, diced
$^1\!/_3$ teaspoon white pepper, crushed
1   star anise
1   bay leaf
2   tablespoons mixed herbs: coriander, chervil, parsley, tarragon, thyme
1   cup quality white wine

Add the diced vegetables to a 2-quart stockpot with enough water (about 4 $^1\!/_2$ cups) to cover the vegetables. Simmer over medium-high heat for about 8 minutes. Add the herbs and spices and simmer for another 2 minutes; then add the wine. Remove the pot from the heat and allow to cool. Place in a storage container and marinate for 48 hours; then strain off the liquid. Yield: About 1 quart. ◆

Béchamel Sauce

Béchamel is a basic white French sauce that is adaptable to many recipes. There are many ways béchamel is prepared. This version goes particularly well with Chef Ian MacDonald's avocado-and-mushroom recipe on page 114. You will need only $^3\!/_4$ of a cup of this recipe for the chef's dish.

1   teaspoon minced onions
1 $^1\!/_2$ tablespoons unsalted butter, plus 1 $^1\!/_2$ tablespoons, cut into bits
1 $^1\!/_2$ tablespoons all-purpose flour
1   cup scalded milk
$^1\!/_8$ teaspoon salt
    White pepper to taste
1   tablespoon freshly grated Parmesan cheese
1   tablespoon grated Gruyère cheese

In a saucepan, cook the onion in 1 $^1\!/_2$ tablespoons of butter over moderately low heat, stirring till soft. Stir in the flour and cook over low heat, stirring for 3 minutes.

Remove from the heat, and add scalded milk in a stream, whisking until the mixture is smooth and thick. Add salt and pepper, and simmer for 5 minutes or until the consistency of a medium cream. Add Parmesan, Gruyère, and butter. Cook over moderately low heat, stirring until cheese and butter are just melted. Remove from heat. If not using immediately, cover the surface of the sauce (not the bowl) with a buttered round of waxed paper. Yield: 1 cup sauce. ◆

Brown Sauce

Recipes often call for a brown sauce, especially red meats and game. You may make this ahead of time as it freezes well. Brown sauce is called a mother sauce because by using it as a base or foundation, many other sauces can be made with the addition of a few new ingredients.

Mirepoix:
- 3 onions, diced
- 4 carrots, diced
- 4 ribs celery, diced

Roux:
- 1/2 cup butter
- 1/2 cup all-purpose flour

Sauce Base:
- 3 quarts homemade beef stock
- 1/2 cup tomato purée

Bouquet Garni:
- 1 bay leaf
- 1 sprig thyme
- 4 parsley stems

Place a large stockpot on the stove with the onions, carrots, and celery. Add the butter, and heat on medium-high. Sauté the vegetables until well browned but not burned. Add the flour and stir to make a roux or paste. Cook the roux until it is browned and the flour cooks away.

Whisk in the stock and the tomato purée and bring to a boil, stirring constantly. Reduce the heat to simmer and skim the surface of any foam or small particles. (Never let the stock come to a rolling boil or the sauce will become cloudy.) Tie together the ingredients for the bouquet garni, using kitchen string. Add the herb bundle to the stock and let simmer for about 2 hours or until the sauce is reduced to about 6 cups. Skim the surface often.

Once reduced, remove the pot from the stove and pour into a strainer lined with several layers of cheesecloth. Press gently on the mirepoix to remove the juices. Chill quickly in a bowl nested inside another bowl of ice water to prevent the spread of bacteria and eliminate the growth of a skin on the surface. Yield: 3 quarts. ◆

Angel-Food Cake

If you do not wish to use prepared sponge or angel-food cake for the Tiramisu recipe on page 191, then here is the recipe for making the cake. When baked, cut to fit the size of the pan in the chef's recipe.

- 1 1/4 cups powdered sugar
- 1 cup cake flour
- 1 1/2 cups egg whites, at room temperature
- 1 1/2 teaspoons cream of tartar
- 1 1/2 teaspoons vanilla extract
- 1/4 teaspoon salt
- 1/4 teaspoon almond extract
- 1 cup sugar

Preheat the oven to 375°. In a small bowl, stir powdered sugar and cake flour. Set aside.

Add the egg whites, cream of tartar, vanilla, salt, and almond extract to a large bowl, and with mixer at high speed, beat until well mixed.

Beating at high speed, sprinkle in sugar, 2 tablespoons at a time until all of the sugar is dissolved and whites form stiff peaks. Do not scrape the bowl during beating.

With a rubber spatula, fold in the flour mixture, about 1/4 cup at a time, just until flour disappears. Pour the mixture into a greased, 8-inch tube pan, and with spatula, cut through the batter, breaking up any large air bubbles.

Bake for 35 minutes or until the top of the cake springs back when lightly touched with a finger. Any cracks on the surface should look dry.

Invert the cake in the pan. Cool completely and loosen from the sides of the pan with a spatula. Yield: 1 cake. ◆

Crème Fraîche

Many recipes — from savories to sweets — call for crème fraîche. The cream is great for cooking in sauces and soups, because it will not curdle. It is also delicious spooned over fresh fruits, fruit cobblers or puddings. Crème fraîche is really a product of France, where the cream is not pasteurized and therefore contains the bacteria necessary to thicken it naturally. In countries such as the United States — where cream is pasteurized — the fermenting agents necessary to make this thick cream, are not present. You can buy crème fraîche in specialty stores in many countries, including America. But it is very costly. The following alternative is a perfect substitute.

(Crème fraîche may be flavored with items such as minced garlic and herbs, horseradish or honey.)

1   cup whipping cream
2   tablespoons buttermilk

Combine the cream and the buttermilk in a screw-top glass container. Cover and let stand at room temperature for 8 to 24 hours, or until the mixture becomes very thick. Stir well and cover. Place in the refrigerator for up to 10 days. ◆

Crème Anglaise

This vanilla custard sauce is useful for many recipes.

12   egg yolks
1   cup sugar
4   cups milk
1   tablespoon pure vanilla extract

In a bowl of electric mixer, combine the yolks and sugar. Beat with the whip attachment until thick and light. In a heavy saucepan, bring the milk and vanilla to boil. With the mixer running on low speed, very slowly pour the milk into the yolk mixture and combine.

Return the milk-and-egg mixture to the saucepan and turn down the heat to medium-low. Heat the mixture slowly, stirring constantly to prevent burning and lumping. Prepare a bowl filled with ice water. When the sauce begins to thicken and coats the back of a wooden spoon, remove the saucepan immediately from the heat and scrape custard into a stainless steel bowl. Place custard-filled bowl into the bowl filled with ice water. Stir the sauce frequently to speed the cooling process. By placing the sauce over ice, the cooling process is sped up and bacteria is less likely to grow. Once the sauce is completely cooled, refrigerate until ready to use. Yield: 2 1/2 pints. ◆

Simple or Sugar Syrup

Simple syrup may be used to poach fresh or dried fruits or berries among other myriad uses.

2   cups granulated sugar
1/2 -1   cup water

In a medium saucepan, bring the water to a boil, stirring to dissolve the sugar. Determine the amount of sugar to use based on the sweetness of the fruits or berries you are using.

Flavor the syrup to match its use. Possible flavorings are: vanilla, wines, liqueurs and other spirits, citrus fruits and peel, and herbs and spices. Yield: 2 cups syrup. ◆

Resource Directory

All of the following companies were hand-picked to be featured in the cookbook and the television show in a variety of ways. Their inclusion in this guide is as a service to the reader.

Athens Pastries and Frozen Foods, Inc.
13600 Snow Road
Cleveland, OH 44142
Phone: (216) 676-8500

World's largest manufacturer of phyllo dough and shells, *spanakopita, baklava,* and other Greek specialties. ◆

Attiki Honey
29 P. Mela Street
12131 Peristeri
Athens, Greece
Phone: (011) 30 1 5717113

One of the largest makers of quality pure honey in Greece. A family-owned business since the nineteenth century, Attiki relies on the flowers upon which the bees feed to produce the varieties of flavorful honeys. ◆

Greek Food and Wine Institute
1114 Avenue of the Americas, 16th Floor
New York, NY 10036
Phone: (212) 221-0572

Information and free copies of *Gastronomia,* a newsletter on Greek cuisine, are available from the Greek Food and Wine Institute. The institute was host to *World Class Cuisine* during the videotaping in Greece. ◆

Minerva olive oil from Krinos Foods stands proudly above the Greek village of Galaxidi.

Inagh Farmhouse Cheeses
Meg and Derrick Gordon
County Clare
Inagh, Ireland
Phone: (011) 353 65 26633

Makers of Irish hard and soft goat cheeses. See Pantry section on page 204 for more information about the farm and cooking with goat cheese. ◆

Ionia Households Industries
8 Dragatsaniou Street
105 59 Athens, Greece
Phone: (011) 30 1 3238762

Maker of fine porcelain used in photos throughout the Greece section and on the front cover. ◆

Ionia dinnerware

D. Kourtakis Wine Producing & Bottling Co.
19003 Markopoulo
Attika, Greece
Phone: (011) 30 299 22234

With wineries situated in the heart of the celebrated wine-growing regions, Attica and Viotia, the D. Kourtakis Company (founded in 1895) blends the traditional with the modern. The company's Kouros label wines were selected for the wine list of the Japanese Silver Bullet train. Kouros is distinguished by its unusual, angled label with a Grecian column. ◆

Krinos Foods, Inc.
33 200
Itea, Greece
Phone: (011) 30 265 32335

Established in 1905, Krinos Foods produces an extensive line of Greek products, including fine olives and olive oils. The company has affiliates in twenty-five countries and a modern factory near Delphi. Krinos was host to *World Class Cuisine* during the videotaping in Greece. ◆

Krinos Foods, Inc. (United States)
47-00 Northern Boulevard
Long Island City, NY 11101
Phone: (718) 729-9000

Krinos Foods, Inc., is reportedly North America's largest importer, distributor, and manufacturer of Greek specialty foods, from frozen and refrigerated to dry goods. Its affiliated plants with state-of-the-art production facilities are in New York, Montreal, and Toronto. Products include Greek olives, olive oils, cheeses, coffees, pastas, fancy foods, and sweets. The recipe testers recommend that cooks use Greek ingredients when preparing the recipes in the Greek section of this cookbook. ◆

Vin de Crete from Kourtakis

Krinos workers in Itea, Greece

Yannis Bournias of Metaxa

Metaxa
6A Metaxa Street
145 64 Kifissia
Athens, Greece
Phone: (011) 30 1 6207100

Makers of world-famous Metaxa Brandy and Ouzo 12. Ingredients come from botanics, especially found on the islands of Greece. ◆

Nestor Imports, Inc.
225 Broadway, Suite 2911
New York, NY 10007
Phone: (212) 267-1133

Exclusive U.S. importer of D. Kourtakis and Calliga wines. ◆

Nicholas Mosse pottery and Waterford crystal complement dessert at Marlfield House.

Nicholas Mosse Pottery
Bennettsbridge
County Kilkenny, Ireland
Phone: (011) 353 56 27105

Ireland's premiere potter, Nicholas Mosse, distributes a classic country line of spongeware designs. Most all pieces are hand-painted and thrown on the potter's wheel. You may find Nicholas Mosse pottery pictured in this book throughout the Ireland section. Some designs are available through the Museum Collections Catalog of Boston. ◆

The Paddington Corporation
One Parker Plaza
Fort Lee, NJ 07024
Phone: (201) 592-5700

Sole U.S. importer of Metaxa spirits and Ouzo 12. ◆

Paterno Imports, Ltd.
2701 South Western Avenue
Chicago, IL
Phone: (312) 247-7070

Exclusive U.S. importer of J. Boutari & Son wines. ◆

Dinnerware from Porta

Porta
225 Fifth Avenue
Suite 927-A
New York, NY
Phone: (800) 822-6026

Makers of many varieties of ceramic and porcelain dinnerware and accent pieces. Porta's production

plant is in Caldas de Rainha, Portugal. Products are featured in fine stores in the United States and Portugal and also in catalogs such as Horchow. Porta provided *World Class Cuisine* with the dinnerware and accent pieces you see throughout the Portugal section. ◆

Classic Malts of Scotland from Schieffelin & Somerset

Schieffelin & Somerset Co.
Two Park Avenue
New York, NY 10016
Phone: (212) 251-8277

Schieffelin & Somerset paired all of the wines with the recipes in this book for the Portugal, England, Ireland, and Scotland sections and helped in the understanding of Scotch whisky in cooking with their line of Classic Malts. The company is an importer for premium wines and spirits such as Moët & Chandon Champagne, Hennessy Cognac, Johnnie Walker Blended Scotch Whiskies, Tanqueray Gin, and Tanqueray Sterling Vodka. The single-malt Scotch whiskies, which they import, are pictured above and on page 140 in the cooking with whisky section. ◆

Shannon Traditional
1443 Palisade Avenue
Teaneck, NJ 07666
Phone: (800) 669-0063

Importers of Irish foods, including Irish bacon. The company sells a full Irish Breakfast by mail order as well. ◆

Titan Food Imports
23-52 48th Street
Astoria, NY 11102
Phone: (718) 626-7771

Leading retailer and national supplier of Greek foods, wines, and spirits. ◆

Ulster Weavers
148 Madison Avenue
New York, NY 10016
Phone: (212) 213-3592

Distributors of fine damask and country-style tea towels, Ulster Weavers showcases a line of linens that reflects the United Kingdom. *World Class Cuisine* used their linens throughout the videotaping in Ireland and some in Scotland. Some of their tea towels may be found in pictures in the Irish and Scottish sections of this book. ◆

Waterford Crystal, Ltd.
Kilbarry
Waterford, Ireland
Phone: (011) 353 51 73311

World-famous, hand-cut crystal has been made here for more than a century. Waterford crystal graces the tables of many *World Class Cuisine* restaurants as seen in the Ireland section of this cookbook in particular. ◆

Directory of Country Houses, Cottage Restaurants, and Hotels

Adare Manor
Adare
County Limerick, Ireland
Phone: (011) 353 61 396566

Amalia Hotel
330 54 Delphi, Greece
Phone: (011) 30 265 82101

Ashford Castle
Cong
County Mayo, Ireland
Phone: (011) 353 92 46003

Auchterarder House
Auchterarder
Perthshire PH3 1DZ
Scotland
Phone: (011) 44 764 663646

Balbirnie House
Balbirnie Park, Markinch
Fife KY7 6NE
Scotland
Phone: (011) 44 592 610066

Braeval Old Mill
Aberfoyle
Stirlingshire FK8 3UY
Scotland
Phone: (011) 44 877 382711

Cashel House
Cashel
County Galway, Ireland
Phone: (011) 353 95 31001

Dromoland Castle
Newmarket-on-Fergus
County Clare, Ireland
Phone: (011) 353 61 368144

Ednam House Hotel
Bridge Street
Kelso
Roxburghshire TD5 7HT
Scotland
Phone: (011) 44 573 224168

Elounda Beach Hotel
721 00 Aghios Nikolaos
Crete, Greece
Phone: (011) 30 841 41412

Fosse Farmhouse
Nettleton Shrub
Near Chippenham
Wiltshire, SN14 7NJ
England
Phone: (011) 44 249 782286

Gleneagles Resort
Auchterarder
Perthshire PH3 1NF
Scotland
Phone: (011) 44 764 662231

Hotel Grande Bretagne
Constitution Square
105 63 Athens, Greece
Phone: (011) 30 1 3230251

Hotel Pentelikon
66 Diligianni Street
GR-145 62 Kifissia, Greece
Phone: (011) 30 1 8080311

Hyde Park Hotel
66 Knightsbridge
London SW1Y 7LA
England
Phone: (011) 44 71 2352000

Kildare Hotel & Country Club (K-Club)
Straffan
County Kildare, Ireland
Phone: (011) 353 1 6273333

Le Manoir aux Quat' Saisons
Church Road
Great Milton
Oxford OX44 7PD
England
Phone: (011) 44 844 278881

Le Meridien Porto
Avenida da Boavista, 1466
4100 Porto, Portugal
Phone: (011) 351 2 6001913

Longueville House
Killarney Road
Mallow
County Cork, Ireland
Phone: (011) 353 22 47156

Marlfield House
Gorey
County Wexford, Ireland
Phone: (011) 353 55 21124

Moyglare Manor
Moyglare, Maynooth
County Kildare, Ireland
Phone: (011) 353 1 6286351

Palace Hotel Bussaco
3050 Mealhada, Portugal
Phone: (011) 351 31 930101

Park Hotel Kenmare
Kenmare
County Kerry, Ireland
Phone: (011) 353 64 41200

Park Lane Hotel
Piccadilly, London W1Y 8BX
England
Phone: (011) 44 71 4996321

Pousada da Rainha
Santa Isabel
7100 Estremoz, Portugal
Phone: (011) 351 68 332075

Pousada de Santa Maria
7330 Marväo, Portugal
Phone: (011) 351 45 93201

The Ritz Inter-Continental
Rua Rodrigo da Fonseca 88
1093 Lisbon, Portugal
Phone: (011) 351 1 692020

Symposio Restaurant
46 Erehtheiou
Makriyanni
117 42 Athens, Greece
Phone: (011) 30 1 9225321

Turnberry Hotel
Turnberry
Ayrshire KA26 9LT
Scotland
Phone: (011) 44 655 31000

Index

The sun sets on another season of World Class Cuisine . . .